Managing outsourcing in library and information services

Sheila Pantry OBE
Peter Griffiths

facet publishing

Sheila Pantry OBE is the editor of The Successful LIS Professional Series and author of *Building Community Information Networks: strategies and experiences*, and (with Peter Griffiths) *The Complete Guide to Preparing and Implementing Service Level Agreements, Creating a Successful e-Information Service, Developing a Successful Service Plan* and *Your Essential Guide to Career Success*.
Peter Griffiths is the author of *Managing Your Internet and Intranet Services: the information and library professional's guide to strategy*. Details of these and other Facet Publishing titles are available at www.facetpublishing.co.uk.

Published by
Facet Publishing
7 Ridgmount Street
London WC1E 7AE

Facet Publishing is wholly owned by CILIP: the Chartered Institute of Library and Information Professionals.

First published 2004

British Library Cataloguing in Publication Data
A catalogue record for this book is available from the British Library.

ISBN 1-85604-543-9

Typeset in Aldine 401 and Syntax by Facet Publishing.
Printed and made in Great Britain by MPG Books Ltd, Bodmin, Cornwall.

Contents

Preface

'Outsourcing' is a term that has been applied during the last quarter of a century to the processes involved in the provision of a service or other business activity to customers by an organization placing its supply in the hands of third parties who are not direct employees.

This is not a new concept, however, and the activity has been taking place on a more partial basis for a considerable time. But outsourcing and the related – frequently synonymous – phrase 'contracting out' have now come to be associated with experiments into the practice of putting entire services in the hands of contractors, rather than distinct parts of that service. This is without doubt an emotive issue, but there is now a considerable body of evidence from various areas of the world suggesting that there are opportunities as well as challenges to be taken into account by library and information professionals considering outsourcing as an option.

Nonetheless outsourcing is often discussed by LIS professionals as if it were a new phenomenon in their industry – yet there are examples that go back over a century. From 1902, the Library of Congress sold duplicate copies of its 5 x 3 inch catalogue cards to libraries around the world, although falling demand from a peak of 78 million cards in 1968 made it no longer viable to produce them.

Library and information services have for many years paid suppliers to carry out routine book servicing tasks, such as labelling or the fitting of plastic jackets. They have made use of services such as the pre-selection of books for inspection or approval, with suppliers providing books likely to fit the criteria of appeal to readers or of price. There is a long tradition in UK libraries of using what are now seen as outsourcing services, but it is only in the context of recent developments that this label has been applied to what were originally simply seen as useful extra buy-in services.

Other support services such as cleaning and maintenance have long been bought in as a result of the development of compulsory competitive tendering (CCT) within local authorities in the UK, and of the decisions made by many public and private bodies to place such work in the hands of facilities management companies.

The resulting impression is that large amounts of library services have been outsourced. In reality outsourcing is now routinely considered as one of the available options when service delivery is being examined as part of an efficiency review. The result, as might be expected, is that a greater amount of business has been outsourced recently, and that the services being outsourced now go far beyond the routine processing of new books, or the supply of pre-printed catalogue cards.

What has been far less common is the contracting out of an entire service, but this possibility has been opened up in the last twenty years, especially in the public sector, by changes in political thinking.

In this book we look at the range of options available to library and information services and draw attention to some of the problems that can emerge. In particular we urge that great attention is paid to the detail of any agreements that may be made, because everyone – customers, suppliers and staff – can be affected by the result.

Each chapter is written to help you through the successive stages of outsourcing. Chapter 1 introduces the concepts of outsourcing and externalization. In Chapter 2 we encourage you to carry out an information audit before any outsourcing is considered, and in Chapter 3 we discuss using the results once the information audit has been completed. The issues of information ownership and using an information provider are considered in Chapter 4.

Chapter 5 looks at how to outsource in detail: selecting the supplier, making the agreement, and handling copyright, licences and the contract period. Chapter 6 advises what to include in the outsourcing agreement – and emphasizes the necessity of full consultation. Chapter 7 expands on the various elements of the agreement, and Chapter 8 suggests ideas for the structure and format of the agreement.

The work does not stop with the agreement being finalized, and Chapter 9 covers how to keep the agreement on target and who should be involved in the process. Keeping customers and staff happy is a delicate balancing act, and all information managers know how vital this is. Chapters 10 and 11 offer a range of strategies for ensuring the success of your outsourced services. Good communications are essential, and in the final chapter we offer some tools to help you get a clear message across at all times.

We hope that the resource list at the end of the book will give you further ideas, and wish you every success in your outsourcing work.

Sheila Pantry OBE
Peter Griffiths

1

LIS outsourcing: an introduction

In this chapter we consider:

- what are outsourcing and externalization?
- how long have they been in use?
- what is the nature of outsourcing?
- why do library and information services outsource?
- what do they outsource?
- what issues arise when outsourcing is carried out?
- what are the effects on customers, staff and suppliers?
- what is the effect on the service?

What are outsourcing and externalization?

There are various definitions of outsourcing and externalization that can be summed up as follows:

> *Outsourcing is allowing another person or organization to provide a service or part of a service previously carried out inside the LIS/organization, usually on a contractual basis.*

Externalization is the delivery of a complete service, including the staffing and possibly the relocation of the service away from the purchaser's premises, by an external supplier.

You will find other definitions in use but they generally amount to the same thing. They make the distinction between the partial and the total delivery of the library and information service (LIS) by a third party or parties.

Outsourcing is a term that has been applied in the last quarter century to the processes involved in the provision of a service or other business activity by placing its supply in the hands of people who are not the direct employees of the organization that provides that service or activity to its own customers. Although, as we shall see shortly, this is not a new concept and the process has been taking place for a considerable time, the term 'outsourcing' and the related – frequently synonymous – phrase 'contracting out' have come to be associated with experiments and practice in putting entire services in the hands of contractors rather than distinct parts of that service. This is without doubt an emotive issue, but there is now a considerable body of evidence from a number of countries that there are opportunities as well as challenges when outsourcing becomes an issue for library and information professionals.

The definition of outsourcing adopted by Resource (now MLA, the Museums, Libraries and Archives Council) is based on one in the American Library Association's publication *Library Technology Reports* and for the sake of consistency we shall adopt it here: 'outsourcing is the contracting of activities to an outside individual or organization (which may be another publicly funded body) in place of the use of in-house staff' (Boss, 1999, quoted by Ball and Earl, 2002). This is very similar to the definition adopted by the American Library Association's ad hoc working party: 'the contracting to external companies or organizations, functions that would otherwise be performed by library employees' (ALA, 2003). It should be sufficiently precise to allow us to start our look at the management and professional issues that outsourcing raises.

2

The background to outsourcing

Outsourcing is often discussed by librarians and information professionals as if it is a new phenomenon in their industry. An important text in this field (Woodsworth and Williams, 1993) places its origins in government privatization policies; a 1994 speaker on the closely allied topic of contracting out (Lawes, 1994) recalled her widely shared first reaction to the idea, that it was a passing management fad – new, by implication – and that it would never last.

Yet there are examples of outsourcing of library and information services that go back over a century. The *Atlantic Monthly* for February 1997 (p.16) reported that 28 February of that year would be the last day that libraries could place orders for catalogue cards from the Library of Congress, ending almost 100 years of service. Since 1902, the Library had sold duplicate copies of its 5x3 inch catalogue cards to libraries around the world, but falling demand from a peak of 78 million cards in 1968 had made it no longer viable to produce them.[1] The Cataloging Distribution Service still provides data to customers, these days using file transfer protocol (FTP) over the internet (having also closed its tape distribution service in 2003 after 31 years), but now concentrates on the primary function of producing and publishing a single authoritative electronic information product rather than being involved in the reproduction and distribution of the data (Library of Congress, 2003).

Libraries and information services have paid suppliers to carry out routine book servicing tasks, such as labelling or the fitting of plastic jackets, for many years. They have made use of services such as the pre-selection of books for inspection or approval, with suppliers providing books likely to fit criteria of appeal to the library's readers or of price. So again there is a long tradition in UK libraries of using what are now seen as outsourcing services, but it is only in the context of recent developments that this label has been applied to what were originally seen as useful services that the library might choose to buy in rather than carry out itself. Other support services such as cleaning and maintenance have been bought in as a result of compulsory competitive tendering (CCT) elsewhere in the local authorities that operate public library services, and following the decisions by many public and private bodies to place building maintenance and cleaning in the hands of facilities management companies rather than continuing to do this work themselves.

The resulting impression is that large amounts of library services have been outsourced, when what may have happened is that outsourcing is now routinely considered as one of the available options when service delivery is being examined as part of an efficiency review. The result, as might be expected, is that a greater amount of business has been outsourced recently, and that the services being outsourced now go far beyond the routine processing of new books, or the supply of pre-printed catalogue cards.

The nature of outsourcing

As has been shown, there is a long tradition of outsourcing low-level processes and the routine parts of some professional activity such as catalogue card production. Far less common has been the contracting out of an entire service, but this possibility has been opened up in the last 20 years, especially in the public sector, by changes in political thinking. At the time of writing only Hounslow public libraries are in this position in the UK, with services provided by a trust under contract to the local authority. A small number of library boards elsewhere in the world have adopted similar policies. However, a number of library services have found themselves in a position where outsourcing has been a possibility or has become a fact, and these range from local authorities, through government departments (where the process was designated 'market testing' in the Government's White Paper *Competing for Quality* (Cabinet Office, 1991)), to libraries in the education sector (Ball and Earl, 2002). Commercial considerations make it more difficult in the corporate sector, where client confidentiality may be a factor weighing against total outsourcing, but even here there are reports of the use of outsourced facilities for storage and other support. Perhaps surprisingly, an extensive list of functions has been outsourced by legal libraries, which would appear to have many of the same concerns (Ebbinghouse, 2002).

CCT has led to some partial outsourcing, such as at the London Borough of Brent, and to situations where parts of a service were outsourced while the core service was still managed in the traditional way as a public service or private company department. In some cases, these trials of outsourcing have since been abandoned.

Outsourcing, externalization and service level agreements

The techniques that we describe in this book will be important in ensuring that outsourcing (or externalization) achieves its purpose under good standards of management. An outsourcing agreement will be essentially the same as a service level agreement (SLA) and can be used to govern the various aspects of the outsourced or externalized service.

However, the service specification must be carefully drawn up, but there are many bridges to cross before this is finally concluded. Especially where the LIS is not consulted, there can be excessive concentration on the quantitative aspects of service (how many books are to be catalogued? how many enquiries are to be handled?) rather than the quality of service (are catalogued books delivered on time? can they be easily found from the catalogue descriptions? do users report satisfactory responses to enquiries?)

The specification must include a mechanism that provides the managers of the outsourced service with access to the policy-making process and the policy makers, so they can stay in touch with the business to receive information on new policies and in order to supply progress reports. A service level agreement is helpful in specifying the arrangements for communications and for managing the flow of information to the service managers.

In this section we have not included recommended wording – see

Chapter 8 for advice on this – but have highlighted the issues that you need to consider. Because the agreements you reach are likely to be contractual in nature, we think it is important that your legal advisers draw up the wording, or approve the agreements that you draft.

The use of outsourcing and externalization

In the UK, many examples of outsourcing and externalization activities trace their roots to the political efforts in the 1980s and 1990s to reduce public sector costs by, for example, the reduction of staff levels.

However, there are earlier antecedents in the USA. Herbert S. White (2000) recalls that the NASA Scientific and Technical Information Facility was completely contracted out to an external supplier in the mid-1960s; one commentator has traced the contracting out of library services in the USA to a 1955 federal government circular (US Bureau of the Budget, 1955).

The literature shows library and information services using outsourcing to help them to grapple with concepts such as 'value for money' and 'best value', and suggests that a justification for outsourcing used by many is that it allows them to focus on their core activities rather than on the delivery of minor services or areas of work that have low value and low interest.

But it can be argued that library and information services have long outsourced many of their activities, and probably for similar reasons. This includes a number of paraprofessional activities such as photocopying, book purchasing, handling journal subscriptions and interlibrary loans. At a more basic level, work such as book jacketing and labelling has been bought in from book suppliers for many decades. Even some professional services such as cataloguing have been bought in for many years, through card supply services (such as the BNB card service) or from electronic suppliers such as OCLC.

Library and information services have also had to manage further developments at the same time as coping with the development of outsourcing:

- cutbacks in funding which have led them to concentrate on core services
- local government reorganization
- growth of LIS purchasing consortia in a number of sectors, e.g. academia
- new business initiatives created by various partnerships, mergers, acquisitions, alliances and sponsorships in the book trade and in library and information services.

There are many examples where outsourcing in the LIS has been achieved with good results:

- security
- cleaning
- catering
- book binding
- loose-leaf updating
- information technology/computer support
- subscription services.

There have been examples in public and private sector libraries where previous in-house providers have competed with private suppliers to offer such services. A frequent, though not universal, experience has been that in-house services have gained greater control of service costs, and there has been a benefit to both the LIS and the organization from the outsourcing process.

Advantages and disadvantages of outsourcing

The LIS that uses outsourcing can find itself in a difficult position if it becomes a (possibly powerless) intermediary between the library user and the library supplier. It will have to put itself first in the position of supplier in order to discover what its users want, and then become the purchaser in order to pass these requirements to the external supplier.

In addition to dealing with this split role, the LIS needs to address some areas of vulnerability which need to be covered in the agreement process.

Minimizing the risk

Identifying areas to outsource requires careful consideration, perhaps at more length than a management anxious for savings is willing to countenance. You do, however, need to ensure that:

- there is a sufficiently large supplier base able to offer the service;
- a large enough number of suppliers are prepared to make a bid at a reasonable price
- you have the resources to manage the resulting agreement or contract.

Otherwise you expose your organization to risk. If you draw up a specification so inflexible that it leads you into a one-to-one agreement with an inexperienced or poor supplier, you have effectively cut off the possibility of any worthwhile service development. Similarly, if you choose to enter an area where there is only one supplier, you are at risk if that company's fortunes fail, and you may be subject to unexpected price rises or shortfalls in service quality. The way of increasing the odds in your favour is to ensure that the specifications you issue for the service are pitched flexibly where necessary. This allows the potential supplier to organize a bid in terms that can be matched against your requirements and to identify possible economies of scale.

Use this book to help you identify these areas for flexibility. Use the growing numbers of SLAs that have been published on the world wide web. Use the period of clarification and negotiation while concluding the contract in order to discover the supplier's strengths and what is already being done for other clients. Try to remove the risks along with the inessential elements of the specification.

You may need to bring in specialist help to arrive at the service definition, for example if you want to outsource web page authoring. Defining the service with this specialist may also help to identify alternative ways of meeting the requirement, or point out that not all the service needs to be outsourced in order to realize your targets.

The question of ownership

In some circumstances, the question of ownership of the service, its stock, and even its staff can arise. Your agreement needs to state this precisely. Because of the nature of this agreement, we reinforce our earlier advice that your legal advisers formulate the words to be used. Common arrangements are:

* Ownership of the stock (infrastructure, etc.) is transferred to the outsourcing company. In this case you need to consider what will happen at the end of the contract period, in order to avoid making an unplanned gift to a contractor you have dismissed. There will need to be safeguards, if you judge them necessary, to prevent the contractor from selling off the stock during the contract period.
* The stock (infrastructure, etc.) is leased to the contractor, possibly for a peppercorn rent. In this way the ownership of the stock is never removed from the LIS. In the public sector this may be the only way that you can outsource.
* The LIS retains ownership of the stock, with the contractor providing personnel or accommodation.

Beware of writing the terms of the agreement so precisely that you prevent the library service from changing its location, or prevent the contractor from disposing of out-of-date reference books.

What to outsource

A recent survey categorizes outsourced areas of LIS work into information technology (IT), technical services, collection development, document delivery, electronic resources and preservation.

Information technology

Libraries often depend on externalized or outsourced IT services. They may be in another part of the organization, or they may be part of a larger agreement with a third-party supplier. Library requirements are often overlooked, where for example the automated library system is run unsympathetically by a supplier that is far more interested in the widespread desktop applications (such as word-processing and spreadsheets) used throughout the organization. Outsourcing library IT may simply be outsourcing an unresolved problem; despite the trend to converged library and IT services in academic libraries, the best protection for the LIS against these problems can lie in ensuring that the service specification for the overall contract contains explicit and well expressed requirements. Specify the IT requirements for the library and information services, records and archives management services, and knowledge or information management as needed, without being browbeaten to define your solutions based on standard software packages.

Internet service providers

A particular aspect of IT outsourcing is the agreement that you are likely to reach with your internet service provider (ISP). You will usually find that you have not a contract but a service level agreement, which will make it more difficult to enforce in law if you get bad service. Service is widely reported to be poor, and ISPs are not keen to place themselves in a position of potential liability. A survey showed that 'SLAs that are met are the exception not the rule. Mostly businesses are not getting the service for which they are paying' (Evers, 2001).

The levels of service quoted often look comfortably high but, because internet service is a 24-hour, seven-day operation, even a small shortfall from 100% connection can translate into uncomfortably long periods of downtime: 99.8% availability allows 17 hours' loss of service in a year. If all 17 hours come together the results could be catastrophic, so it may be wise to insist on an additional clause that limits the length of time that will be tolerated in a single loss of service incident. You are unlikely to regard a time much longer than four hours as too long.

Look at the sample agreements that many ISPs post on the world wide web. You can include useful ideas from these in your own agreement. You may need to insist that you will not sign the standard agreement if its conditions are significantly worse than your requirements dictate.

Technical services

Suppliers are likely to make the running in service specification in this area, since there are many standard services that are bought off the shelf. Physical processing and cataloguing are long established services but non-standard requirements are likely to be charged extra. The market is competitive, but margins are low and suppliers keep their costs down by expecting LIS customers to accept standard products. Nevertheless, we believe it is worthwhile carrying out the specification process in order to identify the true requirements, and to decide whether the standard offer is in fact acceptable.

Collection development

The Liverpool experiment in supplier-led book selection suggests that a specification is highly desirable, perhaps in the form of a published col-lection-development policy indicating core areas and purchasing priorities in terms of types of publication (Naylor, 2000a).

Purchasing consortia are related to this area of work, and to technical services. The techniques of service level management can be useful in drawing up the agreements under which the consortia are set up, and of setting the timescales and other expectations of consortium members.

Document delivery

There is unlikely to be much scope for negotiation in this area, since national document supply services (such as the British Library Document Supply Centre in the UK, or INIST in France) have standard conditions for use, while commercial suppliers such as ingenta also have stated terms of trade. However, a statement of the conditions for use of such services (i.e. guidelines for the choice between purchase and borrowing) could form part of an overall service specification.

Electronic resources

Although some major collections have created published databases from their stock (such as DEVSIS, based on the British Library for Development Studies at the IDS, Brighton), in most cases there is no real prospect of in-house electronic resource creation beyond the normal catalogue. In effect, every consultation of an external database is a small act of outsourcing, and once again it is on the supplier's terms. We look further at this area in Chapter 10.

Enquiry services

For some time now various organizations have outsourced their enquiry services to another organization. The calls to an enquiry service are directed to the supplier organization, which usually has staff trained in the specialism, but sometimes has to reroute back to the main organization because the enquiry needs a more complicated answer. A typical example of this is the UK government's Health and Safety Executive which uses a private company, National Britannia, to operate the HSE public enquiry service which was previously carried out in-house. Interestingly, based on this activity the supplier organization is now supplying an enquiry service to a health and safety professional body. Perhaps the lesson learned here is that there are opportunities for professional information providers to provide the same kind of service.

Preservation

Conservation and preservation are also specialist services where the supplier is likely to have standard terms, and possibly has a better grasp of the technical detail required in the specification. However, there is some scope for setting levels of service in other areas such as restoration or drying services. In case of emergency, the proper treatment of saturated materials may be more important than absolute speed, and the specification (again with expert advice) should reflect the requirements of the LIS.

Negotiating and agreeing the terms
The customers' expectations

An important element in approaching outsourcing is for the customer to understand the effect of outsourcing on service levels. Suppliers may be reluctant to go above particular levels, leading to the users' expectations being disappointed. An agreement should not be concluded with the external supplier until users are fully aware of the service levels being offered, and sign up to them.

A problem encountered at this stage is the need to explain the operation of various areas of library and information work to the LIS users. (Chapter 10 will expand upon this.) While it is always important to keep the users informed when negotiating an agreement for the operation of a LIS service, it becomes more so when services are outsourced. Library users may be expecting a dramatic improvement in service as a result of outsourcing, whereas the time taken to deliver a journal issue from the publisher to the library (or the end-user) will be exactly the same whether the order has been placed by the library or by the outsourced supplier. The only area in this example where any difference can be made is in the time it takes to record the journal's arrival and apply circulation labels.

The LIS user community must understand that although it is, quite rightly, being invited to specify the levels, suppliers may choose to bid a lower level of service, or to negotiate additional costs for the gap between their service bid and the level required. The library manager's task is to ensure that the user community understands these constraints, and that the outsourcing agreement regulates only those areas that can be reasonably influenced by the supplier. Otherwise, there will be an endless stream of pointless enquiries and allegations of poor service, and goodwill among all the parties will be endangered.

The most effective way of negotiation is likely to be through negotiations by the LIS on behalf of the parent organization. If the organization wishes to deal directly with the supplier, try to ensure that you are at least consulted on the wording of the documents before they are put to potential suppliers. The assumption that only librarians/information professionals are capable of understanding the ways of the publications trade is less common than it was, but it is still probably true that many professional purchasers do not intend to become experts on book purchasing and need to be supported by you. Your own interests are best served by a specification that has been 'reality checked' by a LIS professional before issue and which does not create a stream of calls to the LIS manager seeking clarification of terms. Remember that, in cases of doubt, many LIS suppliers still reach for the phone to call a librarian, who will understand what they are saying about the book trade, rather than a professional purchaser in the buying section.

Staff expectations

We discuss the effect of outsourcing on staffing issues in Chapter 11. The threats that are felt when service level agreements are introduced seem even greater when there is the possibility of outsourcing or externalization, and the consequent threat of job losses or radical changes of work patterns or routines. As a result, the process of service specification is highly important in this situation. A precise specification allows members of staff to have a better idea of what should happen under the new arrangements, and provides evidence of what was agreed in negotiation.

The suppliers' expectations

Similarly, the agreement provides the supplier with a record of what was specified and the way in which any outsourced staff would be employed. In the supplier's case too, the record of the negotiated agreement is an important document. The document should indicate to the supplier whether there is a problem as a result of a gap between the customer's expressed requirement and the supplier's own staff and technical resources.

A clear statement in an SLA of a requirement for the LIS to maintain membership of co-operative schemes or other interlibrary organizations may act as a warning to the supplier that negotiation with third parties is required. Statements concerning legal obligations such as the handling of personal data under the Data Protection Act will also highlight areas needing particular attention, and remind suppliers that they need to satisfy you that their procedures will shield you from legal challenge. If the supplier is known to handle information outside the European Union (for example, in order to re-key catalogue card data, which contains personal information), then care should be taken to include a suitable requirement in the agreement.

Providing feedback

Feedback has been identified as a problematic area in outsourcing of services. Particularly if your user committee has been used to detailed monitoring reports, it may demand that the outsourced supplier is monitored to a similar level of scrutiny.

Bear in mind that the more complex the specification and the more performance indicators that are included, the more monitoring activity will fall upon the LIS staff. Monitoring criteria need to be useful as well as meaningful, and simply measured or judged. There are a number of documented instances where the costs of monitoring have outweighed any savings from outsourcing. Indeed there is evidence that where outsourcing is undertaken in an attempt to solve problems in the management chain, or problems of recruitment and retention, these problems are displaced rather than solved. As a result, they become the subject of review meetings with the supplier when performance does not improve.

The supplier may be able to provide a number of standard reports, depending on the service. If there is a quality control system, you should be able to have copies of the output reports that apply to services provided to you. But, if you are being asked to press the supplier to provide bespoke reports, you will need to intervene to protect the supplier's interests.

Normally, a supplier is chosen because of an ability to supply you at lower cost and higher efficiency. Asking the supplier to provide non-standard reports from a bespoke monitoring system will interfere with procedures, and raise costs for you and perhaps for other customers. Persuade your LIS committee to accept standard outputs from the supplier, or ask for a quotation for the supplier to commission further standard reports. Resist efforts to get information that will suit nobody but the library committee, and that is almost certain to spoil the results for everyone.

Throughout this book we stress the importance of regular meetings. These are essential if you outsource in order to build trust between your LIS and the supplier. You will also need meetings with the representatives of your users; but you will have to judge the right moment when (if ever) you decide to let your users near the supplier.

The effect on the service

The overall effect should, of course, be that the library and information service continues to provide the best possible range and quality of service to its users. They, in turn, should be pleased with the levels and quality of the library's service provision.

In fact the nature of the service will change if any degree of outsourcing takes place. With full externalization, the service may come from a different location – in which case the agreement clauses concerning timeliness and the position of service points take on new importance – or with a different staff, who will need to get to know the organization and its members (the library users). With outsourcing, library staff will have to get to know the supplier, and learn how the supplier's products fit into their own range of products for their library users. In either case there is likely to be a change of pace, and it may be as well to build in a period of grace before full levels have to be achieved. For example, the first quarter after the start of a new contract might not be counted towards service credits or penalties. However, users need to be aware of this, and of any amendments to the complaints and escalation procedures during this time. Suppliers are likely to request some such concession even if the purchasing organization does not propose it.

How does the information professional fit into the picture?

Recent moves to outsource services have come as a challenge to the accepted values and the aspirations of many library and information professionals. There is evidence that the changes have both encouraged and disheartened practitioners, with positive responses being most common at middle-management level where the opportunities are both visible and potentially attainable. Junior staff within organizations considering out-sourcing tend to be worried about job security, while more senior managers are concerned at the responsibility the changes bring in terms of their having to take decisions that could adversely affect the careers of those they manage.

The information professional is an essential player in the process of outsourcing. He or she is the link that interprets the value of the library and information service to the organization's management. In an organization that has determined to outsource its information service, the professional's role is first to ensure that the specification for the new service fully meets the organization's requirements; then to ensure that the supplier selected is capable of meeting that requirement (and does so). Whether or not the in-house team is selected to provide the service, it alone has the skills and knowledge to specify the organization's needs. Specification of services requires particular skills. If there is any suggestion that it will be possible for generalist staff or external consultants to draw up this specification without drawing on in-house professional expertise, that suggestion should be resisted.

Librarians and information professionals do not necessarily have the skills to specify service requirements, but they are not difficult to learn. Common sense plays a great role, both in terms of defining what needs to happen, and how the purchasing organization will recognize that it has happened to a satisfactory standard (so that money can change hands). Library and information professionals need, in effect, to define what libraries do in such a way that someone else can evolve a means of doing it on their behalf. (Note that it is not important to define *how* that outcome should be achieved; that is for the supplier to decide. Note too that it is entirely open to any prospective supplier to decide to employ library and information professionals to help to interpret the requirement and define the response.) People writing specifications need to examine the activities of the existing service (we look at information audit techniques in

Chapter 2) and decide which elements are indispensable, which are desirable but not essential, and which might be attractive at the right price. The specification will eventually reflect all these points, will be written in clear language that will communicate to other professionals what the organization wants, and will allow the in-house professional to make a fair assessment of the bids in order to select the best.

Finally, the library and information professional needs to secure a role as adviser. It is one thing to help procure a supplier's services but, if the supplier then turns out to be submitting poor or late work, there needs to be a mechanism in place to provide informed professional criticism that obtains an improvement to the required standard, a warning or ultimately the installation of an alternative provider who is up to the job. It's worth making sure that the organization is aware that in the event of total failure of the supplier (and they do sometimes close down as well as fail), it might have to depend on the remaining in-house professional team setting up a service at short notice and reverting to earlier supply arrangements.

The clear designation of this role using a term such as 'intelligent customer' makes it clear that it is equally essential in the library and information service arena to have this specialist role as it is in information technology, where it is widely accepted.

So these developments are a real challenge to library and information professionals, but by being willing to adopt new roles there is a clear path forward. The manager will need additional skills to keep all staff informed and motivated during the outsourcing process, and this is no easy task. But, with comparatively little call for new skills from any good LIS manager, a new and positive role that derives from outsourcing can be identified.

Summary

This chapter has taken an overview of some of the issues raised by outsourcing and externalization of library, information and related services. We have seen that outsourcing on a small scale has been happening for decades, and that even total externalization is not a new idea. But it is important to have good specifications of services, and to ensure that where internally supplied services remain, the staff are consulted in reaching the service specification statement. It needs to be recognized that all parties – staff, users and suppliers – should be involved, and that services will undergo change as a result.

Outsourcing can produce worthwhile savings, and improve the quality of the remaining staff, but it also has the potential to go badly wrong when requirements are not clearly spelt out, and negotiated and agreed by all parties.

Note

1   Even at this early date, it was not only permitted but mandated by law that the Library of Congress would generate income from its cataloguing and other publishing activities: 2USC 150, the law giving authority for the services, stated: 'The Librarian of Congress is authorized to furnish to such institutions or individuals as may desire to buy them, such copies of the card indexes and other publications of the Library as may not be required for its ordinary transactions, and charge for the same a price which will cover their costs and ten percentum added, and all moneys received by him shall be deposited in the Treasury and shall be credited to the appropriation for necessary expenses for the preparation and distribution of catalog cards and other publications of the Library.'

2

Be brutal:
the information audit

In this chapter we look at:

- what needs to be addressed before outsourcing is considered
- organizational needs
- information audit and consultancy
- arguments to convince undecided management
- outcomes
- reputation management.

Questions to ask before outsourcing

Information services should be central to every organization irrespective of the sector – academic, government, workplace, public, legal, financial, technical, scientific or medical. There should be a time in the existence of all information services when questions are asked about image, role, function, effectiveness and cost benefit to users. It is equally important to do this when building electronic services for, sometimes, an invisible audience.

Before any form of outsourcing is considered, an information service must review its current situation. What quality systems are in place? What is the level of staff knowledge and experience? What products does the service provide, and what is in its future business plan? It will need to be brutal in its appraisal of its services and systems and must strive to improve, through staff training and innovation, and through constantly asking questions such as:

- What is the core business?
- How are we doing?
- Why is each job done? Does it need to be continued? Can the need for it be avoided?
- How is it done? Why this way? Can a better way be found?
- When is it done? Why then? Can a better time be found?
- Where is it done? Why there? Can a better place be found?
- Who does this job? Why is it done by them/him/her? Is there someone else, inside the organization or outside, who can do this job?
- Are the staff able to deliver the services/products? What training will be needed?

Where the question has begun with the word 'Can?' ask it again with the word 'Should?' This will open up two further issues for decision, depending on the answer to the question containing the word 'Can?' If the answer was 'No', is it worth investing to find out whether a way can be found to do things better? If the answer was 'Yes', does it follow that the service should go to the alternative supplier or means of providing the service? The process is likely to be uncomfortable, as the assumed answer until now has usually been 'Everything's fine, thanks.' In the present business climate, you will have to show that not only is all truly excellent, but that you have looked at other ways of doing things excellently and made a balanced decision that yours is better.

In order to achieve the highest quality of service and the best performance targets you will have to make your customers aware that they too have a role to play. Customers should:

- be aware of what the information service can do

- identify their information problems/needs
- agree to bring them to the information service as first port of call
- communicate them to the information service staff and discuss them as required
- give feedback to the information service
- keep information service staff aware of their changing subject interests
- involve the information service in projects that have information implications.

At the end of the day it is the customer who really decides the quality of the services, by:

- making demands for improvements on an existing service
- asking for new services
- showing a willingness to co-operate.

The customer may need help in order to be able to contribute. The tool by which this is done is an information audit, which has equal potential in public service and in academic environments as in the special library services where it was first developed. It is an important and valuable technique that yields data about the information resources held within the organization or community, its match to the information requirements of the customer group, and the opportunities for intrapreneurial behaviour. In creating a successful information or electronic information service the LIS manager will need to carry out such an information audit which makes people stand back and analyse why, how, where and what exactly the information service is trying to achieve. There will be ample opportunities to develop services once this knowledge is acquired.

Organizational needs

An important task for information managers is to get a clear understanding of the entire organization or community in which the service will operate. Without this understanding the library and information service will not achieve a central role in the user community. A LIS that is driven by a vision shared only by its own staff will never be seen as important by the organization it serves.

Irrespective of the subject background, the organization's or the client's needs should be identified and captured before work begins on any alteration to the service, or the identification of the electronic components within it. The first step is to carry out an information audit of the organization's information needs. It should aim to discover the purpose to which information is put, in case this reveals more effective alternative sources.

Information audit and consultancy

An information audit provides the organization with a wealth of important data such as:

- what information exists within the organization
- where it is located
- how many sections within the organization or the community being served have their own collections of information, or have an official branch of the information service
- what information the organization needs and when it is needed
- who uses it
- what gaps exist
- where potential customers for information are in the organization
- why people use a particular service or source of information in preference to others
- why some people use the service frequently or occasionally
- why some people never use the service
- how to produce the information in the format needed
- what training is needed for both staff and users.

Armed with this data, the LIS manager can begin to put together the range of services that will meet the needs of the greatest number of users in the most cost-effective way. But remember that it can take considerable time from initial consultation and information audit to the final outcomes in the form of revised services or products when any outsourcing work can start. A consultation exercise carried out at the UK Royal College of Nursing is reported to have taken a full two years (Hyams, 2001).

To obtain the data, the LIS manager should hold discussions with managers or other representatives (depending on the type of community being served) to gather details of the types of information that members of that community need. The exercise should provide a clear understanding of the ways that users currently access information, and of the types of information they use.

As well as revealing what kind of information is needed, who needs it, and the range of topics that must be covered, the information audit will also show requirements for any kind of information that is not currently available in the organization. The audit questionnaire will identify any regular specialist information needs together with systems and service being used to meet those requirements. In our books *Creating a Successful e-Information Service* (2002), *Developing a Successful Service Plan* (2000) and *Becoming a Successful Intrapreneur: a practical guide to creating an innovative information service* (1998), we explain these ideas in more detail.

Typical questions and activities that can help identify requirements include:

- Which information resources do you believe support the organization's aims and objectives and its programme of work? What information, for a commercial concern, supports its products and its markets?
- Can you categorize these information sources into the following groups: essential, desirable or nice to have?
- Where (in which departments) does the information reside?
- How up to date is it, and how is it maintained (both its contents and to ensure all copies are the same)?

25

- Where are the gaps in existing information flows and currently held information?
- As well as these gaps, what other major information needs exist?
- How many different computer-based information systems are in use already?
- How many people in the community use externally based information services already, e.g. online databases, the internet, CD-ROMs?
- Are all community members fully trained and able to use the computerized services and technologies?
- If not, how much training is needed and at what level?
- Finally, ask individuals the question: 'On what information do you depend to carry out your job (or any regular activity in the community)?'

Problems

The information audit is likely to reveal a number of problems to be tackled. Below are common problems, although you may find others that are specific to your organization or community:

- Information is power – so there may be a limited sharing of information. In an organization, sections or departments may hoard information, but it can easily be individuals in a community or corporate body who do this without involving others, even if they work in the same area.
- Sections and individuals may have developed databases but may not have taken a co-ordinated approach. Information may be fragmented as a result, or else duplicated without it always being apparent that this has happened.
- Out-of-date information may be in use; or information which has not been checked for validity and authority.
- Worse, an organization or community may be paying to acquire out-of-date information without realizing that it is inaccurate and largely

valueless. This behaviour can lead to costly delays and to policy errors if the wrong source is eventually chosen and acted on.

- Members of the community may suffer telecommunications problems such as a lack of e-mail facilities.
- Staff may lack training in information skills – they may be information illiterate.
- A community may acquire the same or closely similar information several times over through lack of co-ordination between various groups of actors.

Defining information resources and services

In our book *The Complete Guide to Preparing and Implementing Service Level Agreements* (2nd edn, 2001), we urge the use of a glossary or other agreed list of definitions to avoid any question of ambiguity over the questions asked in the audit or the interpretation.

In the context of electronic information services, the areas detailed below will need particular attention. We have found considerable evidence that many managers understand neither the issues that information professionals have to deal with in purchasing and managing information, nor the terminology we use to describe those activities. Many terms have multiple definitions and multiple meanings that must be defined.

The problem goes even wider. As information professionals we often seek the endorsement of other managers for our activities, but they do not understand the consequences of what we seek to do. Imagine the situation reversed: would you sanction a major reorganization of a financial or legal service if you had no idea what the service was providing and the description was ambiguous or meaningless, or couched in financial jargon you did not understand?

An information audit will seek to answer a number of questions about information and its use in the organization. It will pose a number of questions that should convince management (or the people funding the service) of the value of time and effort spent on the information audit activity. And it will consider a number of problems that may be met in the organization's behaviour in the use of information.

Arguments to convince undecided management

What if you need to convince management that an information audit, which can be costly in time and effort, is needed? You need to ensure that the organization can answer positively all these questions if it is to assure others that it has no need for an audit. In each case, in parentheses, is the question that might apply in a public sector or local authority service:

- Are you certain that you have effective control of information resources and the organization's expenditure on them (or, in the public sector, the budget which funds them)?
- Can you define the organization's main information needs and say whether they are satisfied? (Or, what are the client group's main information needs and does the service satisfy them?)
- How many different computer-based information systems exist already and what information do they contain? Is the information reliable and compatible? Would they all provide the same accurate answer to a given question? What do your major customers already use as information services? Do they provide reliable information? Are you holding different answers to their questions?
- How many staff use external information services already, e.g. online databases, the internet, CD-ROMs? Are these better than internal sources? What external information services do you – and your customers – have access to? Do you have, or need, a budget?
- Are all staff members fully trained and able to use the computerized services and technologies?

Outcomes

By carrying out an information audit the manager will be able to:

- understand how the library and information service and products are perceived – or not!
- determine and describe the organization's real information needs
- find out where the library and information service's customers are in the organization
- understand why people in the organization go elsewhere for information
- identify who really needs information
- know how to provide the information when it is needed
- understand the importance of producing information in the format customers need
- use the results of the information audit in any future publicity.

The information professional who has such an understanding and appreciation of these issues is far better able to provide a service which is relevant in the eyes of the senior managers and other influential figures in the organization.

Once the information audit has been initially completed then the rethinking and discussion about any outsourcing of the service(s) can go ahead in the knowledge that the information service will be providing what the customers need and want.

Reputation management

One new area where the information professional has a particular contribution to make is in reputation management. The concept has developed recently but encompasses two things that we have been doing for a long while. One of these is ensuring that the quality and reputation of the services within the organization remain at the highest possible level, and the other is looking after the good name of the organization and the services within it across the wider scene. Branding and quality management are important elements of the first activity, while the second develops into the area sometimes known as 'competitive intelligence' or even 'information warfare'.

In a branding context, the manager will need to ensure that reputation management is built into the organization. It is no good starting an information service (or any other service) without the knowledge that its service levels and quality can be sustained – not just this month or even this year but as an ongoing part of the whole service. The reputation of the manager, the staff and the type of service that is delivered are all at stake, while customers must be reassured that any product bearing the label of the information service meets standards of quality, accuracy and rigour. This is no more than should be required within any organization that possesses a service quality certification (e.g. EN 9000). An information manager has a double role: to provide the quality of service that will maintain the organization's reputation but also to use the processes that the information service develops for this reason in order to assure the internal reputation of the service, and thus remove the need for other parts of the organization to develop duplicate services.

Intriguingly, the concept of reputation management first developed in an area of the information profession's work, even though it has now been taken on and developed by management consultants. The internet usability expert Jakob Nielsen is credited with the first widely accepted definition: the reputation manager in the original definition would co-ordinate large numbers of quality judgments provided by users of a service. By 1999, Nielsen's definition was:

> an independent service that keeps track of the rated quality, credibility, or some other desirable metric for each element in a set. The things being rated will typically be websites, companies, products, or people, but in theory anything can have a reputation that users may want to look up before taking action or doing business. The reputation metrics are typically collected from other users who have had dealings with the thing that is being rated. Each user would

indicate whether he or she was satisfied or dissatisfied. In the simplest case, the reputation of something is the average rating received from all users who have interacted with it in the past.

There are two ways for users to decide whether they want to use the information service on offer:

- **Brand:** the user knows that the service usually provides certain qualities; if the user likes these qualities, then it will probably be worth visiting and using time and time again.
- **Reputation:** the user follows the advice of *other* users who know that the service has quality that is consistent, or the user is influenced by comments published by third parties.

Information professionals were involved in the creation of the discipline of reputation management; their skills will help to maintain both their reputation within your organization and your organization's reputation in the market place. But there is a further way of using the information professional's skills, which is to monitor your reputation, sharing what is found and ensuring that action is taken to remedy any untrue statements.

Users take account of both the organization's reputation and that of its information service in deciding, for example, whether to use information from the web without further corroboration, and services that collaborate with your information service take reputation partly into account when deciding the degree to which they will work in co-operation with you.

And, to square the circle finally, the modern information professional will be eager to acquire the reputation of being able to work in this field. While this presents the manager with a problem of staff retention, it also highlights the importance of reputation at a personal as well as a corporate level.

Building customer loyalty and keeping it

Experience of building information services, and electronic products and services and keeping customers over many years has given us an insight into the behaviour of customers:

- They like to be consulted before, during and after the service or product has been produced.
- They like customer care in all its aspects: e-mails, telephone calls, focus groups, etc.
- They tell others – this is where reputation management kicks in.
- They let you know what the competition is doing, and how well.
- They tell you what is new that should be included in your product.
- They like to have contact with a staff member they know – similar to account managers in the public relations and marketing world.
- They do not like change without consultation. In managing change staff and users alike must be carried along.

The effects of outsourcing

These characteristics mean that a big issue when outsourcing an existing information service or part of it is to keep in touch with users' and staff perceptions. But, because the information audit will have involved these and other 'stakeholders' in discussion, there should be goodwill and even enthusiasm and ready-made loyalty for the information service that will assure users that any changes have been well thought out and thoroughly discussed.

This does not remove the need to communicate reasons for outsourcing, which could be:

- a response to the information audit findings
- to get closer to users' needs
- to take advantage of the latest technologies.

There is more about communication in Chapter 12.

Summary

It is essential to look closely at the organization's information needs and consult with all the stakeholders before any work is carried out on outsourcing. The information audit and subsequent consultation may well provide some surprises but they will verify the need for high-quality information services that satisfy the customers' needs. Whatever the needs, remember that many people do not like change: the information manager will have another challenge in gaining users' acceptance if the decision is to outsource services, or to provide new ones using an external provider.

3

When to outsource: using the results of the information audit

In this chapter we look at the decisions to be made about outsourcing:

- using the results of the information audit
- what types of service should be outsourced?
- how to meet special requirements of particular sectors
- why information services outsource (or don't).

Using the results of the information audit

In Chapter 2 we had an overview of the techniques of information audit. The result of the audit for your organization is likely to be a document – probably some kind of spreadsheet or table – that will identify:

- users of your current services
- the level of take-up you are experiencing for each service
- where you are putting effort into services that nobody is using
- the need for services you are not providing.

In terms of outsourcing, each of these categories requires you to do some evaluation. The first category might seem simple: your customers use the service that you provide – what could be a simpler case to go on doing the right thing? Well, that could be the situation. But what if the 'wanted' list includes a service that you have always wanted to provide, or one that you have always promised you would get round to starting as soon as the demand for other services fell back a little and gave you the capacity to do so? Is it still the best idea to put your effort into doing the same things? What would happen if you chose to outsource one of the current well used services and used the time and expertise saved in order to kick-start the new service? You need to know that if you decide to go on doing your popular services yourself, it's because you have demonstrated that this is the most effective way of doing so. (Don't feel that you have to throw out everything you currently do – it may be a real problem to pass on your internal knowledge to an external contractor, and commercial sensitivity may prevent you doing so. Just be sure that this is the way you want things.)

Assuming that you have reviewed the core list, what about the other two categories? What are you currently doing that your customers do not value? There are several options:

- One is to shut down the service. Information professionals and librarians tend to dislike doing this, as they feel that someone somewhere must be able to make use of it and, if the service is maintained long enough at sufficiently high quality, somebody influential will find it and recommend it to everyone in the organization. Actually, this doesn't happen very much, and one good test is to ask 'Could I justify buying this service for the library if it came from an external supplier?' If the answer is that it doesn't make good sense to buy the service, it's almost never good sense to go on doing it yourself. Of course you could charge your customers for the service, and then either continue it in-house, or use the income to outsource the work.

- Another option is to outsource but to absorb the costs yourself, which means that the service would have to pass your value-for-money assessment to receive funding, and could well fail the questions in the paragraph above.

- If you feel that the service is valuable but underused, then you have
  an option that is nothing to do with outsourcing, which is to give it
  proper publicity and to sell it to the people who should be using it,
  rather than waiting in vain for that key decision-maker to stumble across
  it and promote the service for you.

By the time you get to services that people want but that you don't provide, you should be getting into your stride. You will know whether you
have the capacity to do the work in-house, especially as you have been
taking a ruthless look at your existing services and deciding whether to
keep them, and whether to outsource them. Are you now going to use
those freed-up resources to set up new services that meet the expressed
needs of your users as reflected in the information audit? Here too there
are options to consider:

- In-house provision may well represent good use of the resources available.
- But are there more requirements than resources? In particular, is there
  demand for a new service where your resources (your expertise, your
  staff, your collection, your selection of journal subscriptions, etc.) would
  make or break the new service? If so, services like these are the place
  that any spare resources should be put.
- For other services, you should assess the potential for outsourcing as
  a way of providing the service, and possible funding models to pay for
  it.

Types of outsourced services

We have described a number of types of service that are commonly outsourced in the library and information services domain, but here is a list
of services that have been outsourced with reportable results, positive or
otherwise. The range varies enormously, from complete services to small
component parts:

- entire library services, e.g. Haringey, Invercargill (Harrington, 2003)
- business information services, e.g. Birmingham (Business Insight, 2003; Assinder, 2004)
- business research (Business 360 reports; Freshminds and others)
- public enquiry services, e.g. UK Health and Safety Executive
- school library services, e.g. Dorset (Ball and Earl, 2002)
- buildings, e.g. Bournemouth, Brighton, Newcastle-upon-Tyne – see Chapter 5
- cataloguing, e.g. Library of Congress and British National Bibliography, Interlib, OCLC and other examples
- journal supply (various)
- book selection, acquisition, processing and shelf-ready presentation: numerous examples worldwide, e.g. see discussions on PUBSIG-L New Zealand discussion list
- library management software, e.g. Essex (Ball and Earl, 2002)
- looseleaf document updating.

Outsourcing by sector

A number of factors affect the way that various sectors of information work have taken up outsourcing as a policy.

The public sector

In the public sector there has been political pressure to undertake reviews of the potential to outsource services – whether these have been described as 'best value reviews' or 'market tests' – but the conclusion has been that the market as a general rule is not able to offer services that allow the total contracting out of a public sector library service. Nonetheless, there are recent examples of contractors managing major services, such as Instant Library's tenure at Haringey Libraries, Archives and Museums Service, established in July 2001. In 2003 the service was the runner-up (to

Manchester City Council's management of the 2002 Commonwealth Games) in the *Local Government Chronicle* award for the best public–private partnership (PPP) of the year, with the citation:

> In a best value inspection in early 2001, Haringey's library service was judged to be poor. Serving one of the most deprived communities in the country, this damning report marked a watershed for the council, triggering it to look at a radical new way to run this key service.
>
> By July, the UK's first PPP for a library service was born and, in just over a year, has brought about some remarkable results.
>
> Since the partnership with Instant Library was set up, visitor numbers are up by a staggering 57%, bucking the national trend.
>
> There have been extensive repairs and refurbishments, a major upgrade in IT, longer opening hours, and the acquisition of an extra £200,000 of new materials.
>
> In addition, a new staffing structure, coupled with training and development, is unleashing the true potential of staff, making them more customer focused. Haringey's library service is critical to achieving the council's long-term aim of regenerating socially excluded neighbourhoods.
>
> www.lgcnet.com/awards2003/short_public.htm

The central government sector

In the central government sector there has been outsourcing of one kind or another for over 25 years, ranging from the Interlib project of the late 1970s and early 1980s (an early example of centralized computer-based cataloguing supplied by an external agency, the British Library) to the market tests of the 1990s which led to some radical changes in the way that some departments' library services were managed. The role of suppliers changed from supplying the library to supplying the library's customers, and supplying the library on a similar basis to all other customers. Services such as journals consolidation became an increasingly attractive alternative to managing journals in-house. But views were also expressed that the benefits were insufficient to warrant the outlay in terms of money and staff disaffection (Burge, 1998).

The business sector

Recent research in the business sector suggests that there is no particularly consistent approach to outsourcing (Business 360, 2003 and 2004 forthcoming). Around half of the organizations surveyed do not have a formal policy on outsourcing and many approach outsourcing opportunities on an ad hoc basis. Where policies exist, they are concerned with reducing costs and headcount but, as contracts continue, the emphasis shifts to quality and reliability of service, although the surveys show this is an objective cited only by around a third of respondents. In effect, only a few companies outsource a major element of their research and information effort: a common reason is to manage periods of peak demand, or to cope with downsizing of the in-house research function. The decision to outsource seems generally to be a deliberate one: only 1% of the 2003 survey reported outsourcing in response to a cold call. In the final analysis, outsourcing is still an unusual event in this sector too, with many more organizations outsourcing their travel agency arrangements rather than their information and research functions.

Why information services outsource (or don't)

The survey undertaken by Business 360 in 2003 looked at the concerns of the participating information services when outsourcing. The most common area for concern was in ensuring that consistent and acceptable quality was obtained, followed by ensuring that the outsourced supplier understood the question and produced relevant results in response. Others were worried that the service might not be available when they needed it. A further group of concerns focused on transactions and relationships with suppliers, including pricing, billing and feedback.

Respondents identified benefits too: outsourcing allowed their in-house staff to work on higher value operations, as well as bringing them financial savings and giving them improved staff coverage at off times. However, the benefits were offset by additional concerns, such as the effect on career prospects, salaries and job security.

The overall results were fairly pessimistic about outsourcing of research, with many thinking that falling quality and rising costs were likely to go together; the general view being that the current levels are likely to remain for the next two years. Outsourcing of services will remain useful on an ad hoc basis, although around 20% of the 2003 sample thought that the work involved was too great in comparison with its small perceived value. But this view was not shared by those who already had significant experience of outsourcing: they were far more positive about the process, felt less threatened by it, and saw benefits because the use of external researchers allowed the in-house team to use their 'local' knowledge to best effect.

Compare the results of the Business 360 survey with those claimed by Business Insight, a service based at Birmingham Central Library and which originated as the commercial library founded in 1919. Here, customer benefits from outsourcing are claimed as:

- new business services at minimal cost
- personal one-to-one enquiry service
- savings on staff training costs
- informed decisions
- revenue savings.

While most of these reflect the findings of the Business 360 survey, it's interesting that some of the services there found that their training costs increased, because they had to train existing staff in new ways of working that made most effective use of the outsourced providers' service.

Summary

We have considered how you can use the results of your information audit to determine the most fruitful areas of your service that could be outsourced. We have then looked at the experiences of library and information services in various sectors, and at the advantages and disadvantages found by surveys of customers and claimed by outsourcing providers. Finally, the references in this chapter provide further reading and information that will allow you to research areas of particular interest.

4

Information ownership and using an information service provider

In this chapter you will find details about the following:

- who owns information?
- using subscription agents and other information service providers.

Information ownership

In the past it was relatively easy for the LIS, irrespective of sector, to know who owned information. You bought printed journals and magazines, books, reports, conference proceedings, translations, handbooks and encyclopaedias, etc., and mostly they contained information stating the publisher and address, the year of publication, and the edition with a copyright statement. Once purchased, the documents themselves, but not the copyright, belonged to the LIS until a decision was made to either ditch the item or relegate it to the store for archiving.

Now, in the electronic age, it is sometimes very difficult to know who actually owns the information – the author, the organization, the committee, the publisher, the aggregator, the Crown? Even when authorship is declared the LIS and any outsourced service provider can run into difficulty.

Take the following example: when an LIS purchases an annual electronic subscription for a journal, is this now 'owned' by the LIS as if it were a printed annual subscription which resides in the library or information centre? Some guidelines need to be established and clearly understood by both staff and users if the LIS is going to outsource the subscriptions to journals.

Authority to reuse

Getting authority for the reuse of information is therefore one task too many for many organizations. The draft European Union Directive on the reuse of public sector information is likely to bring about some radical changes in the way that organizations can use local and central government data in the future. But it seems that the effect may well vary between countries in Europe and it will become a complex matter to locate comparable sources of information, establish the conditions for use, and create a value-added product that complies with those restrictions and permissions. The use of a specialist agent looks like a sensible approach to such a complex problem: while it may not prevent a mistake being made, the customer can be reassured by using an agent with known expertise backed by suitable indemnity insurance.

The existence of collecting societies – primarily the Copyright Licensing Agency, the Newspaper Licensing Agency and the Educational Recording Agency – provides you with a ready-made solution to many of the issues around a range of published materials. By using their services, you effectively outsource and avoid the need to reach individual agreements with authors, publishers, broadcasters and performers.

Freedom of Information Act 2000

Many organizations in the UK will be affected by the Freedom of Information Act 2000 (FOI), which becomes operational for most public bodies in January 2005. After this time there will be a worldwide and retrospective right to request the supply of any information held within a public body. The management issues around the supply of internal information fall outside the scope of this text but, if you are affected by this Act, you should be able to identify the ownership of any information that you hold after January 2005, so that you can ensure that you are not breaching copyright or other intellectual property rights when you supply information in response to FOI enquiries.

The simple message is that whatever the approach that you take, you must be certain that your use of third-party information complies with legal and contractual obligations.

Using an information service provider

Not everyone likes or feels competent to negotiate electronic information licences with their providers. For many it is a step too far from the traditional print agreements, and these licences are complicated by being subject to the law of contract under the copyright provisions. Many LIS professionals do not have the skill and expertise to sort out a large number of contracts with a range of information providers and publishers across the world. Knowledge of copyright agreements and the laws of several parts of our global village are new demands on so many of us. Various organizations can procure access rights to digitized information on behalf of their client – the LIS – from wherever they are in the world (and wherever the information is). And, because these organizations are usually global themselves, they know and understand the law as it stands in the country of a document's origin.

There are different types of outsourced providers:

- Some are rewarded by both the client organization and by the information provider. For example, a bookseller buys from a publisher and gets a percentage discount but then charges the client the full price or offers a reduced level of discount.

- Other outsourcers work as a branch of the client organization and are paid a fee for providing services such as journal subscriptions. Alternatively, they may negotiate savings and be paid on a percentage basis.

The agents in these examples do not own the information but, by using their services, subscribers can save a number of internal staff posts that would otherwise have to be employed on this work. The remaining staff can then be switched to more interesting information service provision.

External agents offer a range of further services such as:

- representing consortia or funding bodies in negotiation
- providing centralized administrative and payment services
- formulating e-content strategies
- defining plans for content migration.

The case study gives an insight into what a typical service provider, Swets Information Service, can offer:

Case study What Swets Information Service can offer as a service provider

Swets Information Service is one of the world's leading subscription and information services companies. It is constantly looking at ways to develop tools that will help LIS managers achieve their targets.

Among the services that Swets offers its customers are:

- e-journal license brokering for multi-site and multinational organizations, academic consortia and any organization that does not fit, or does not accept, publishers' standard license terms, conditions (and prices)
- payment administration – from thousands of libraries to thousands of publishers, regardless of location or currency
- claims management
- print processing – Swets offers a 'consolidation' service which means that it takes over the routine processing of print journals and delivers them serviced ready for circulation.

Swets announced in March 2004 that it had launched a far-reaching drive to further simplify the management of electronic journals for customers. Its SwetsWise Title Bank is the first new tool to be developed as part of this drive and is launched in Summer 2004. It allows clients to customize their entire list of electronic subscription links whether they originate from external databases, publishers' websites or SwetsWise Online Content. It also assists customers in maintaining optimum control of their electronic resources, providing maximum full-text access to all titles. Features include the ability to browse title and subject lists, conduct title and subject searches and consult both title and article-level usage data.

Swets described its goal in launching its e-journal management drive as being to simplify the entire chain of complexities from administration to accessing. SwetsWise Title Bank's value lies in giving users one clear picture of where they can access their entire electronic and print content. At the same time, it requires minimal maintenance, allowing customers to easily pass on the full benefits of e-subscriptions to their end-users.

Swets Print Subscription Management

Managing numerous subscriptions from a wide variety of publishers is no simple task, and the administration involved can be both time-consuming and labour-intensive. In its Print Subscription Management, Swets acts as the customer's single point of contact for acquiring and managing all subscriptions. This relieves the LIS of the task of managing subscriptions and allows it to concentrate on core activities instead. This service comprises:

- search and select – title availability, pricing information and new title alerts from the supplier's database
- quotations for subscription prices
- order placement
- subscription renewal checklists
- subscription cancellations
- consolidated invoicing, budget splits and financial risk management

- claim processing for missing issues
- reporting: comprehensive and flexible management reports
- informing all publishers of changes
- electronic data interchange (EDI) – fast and error-free electronic delivery and information processing (claiming, invoicing, ordering, e-check-in)
- dedicated customer service.

The benefits to the LIS

This service offers a number of potential benefits to an LIS. The system provides a clear profile of the library's subscription requirements, allowing it to efficiently and effectively fine-tune them. The LIS can streamline administration processes, enabling it to identify duplication and waste, saving time and costs.

The service provides a single point of contact for all the library's subscription management needs, and provides a single, specified invoice for all your subscriptions, rather than receiving separate invoices for each and every publication, which again reduces costs. The agent in this example has to work closely with 65,000 publishers worldwide to continuously update the subscription information in its database of over 265,000 titles.

Consortia & Multi-site Management: helping you plan, implement and manage special e-journal deals

Outsourced services can also help library and information professionals manage access rights, licensing arrangements and price negotiations. Swets Consortia & Multi-site Management helps organizations achieve optimum access to electronic content. This is a modular service with a number of elements that the customer can choose to implement:

- planning and consultancy – facilitating consortial and organizational objectives, requirements and reporting needs

- brokering – providing quotes, negotiating with publishers and resolving licensing issues
- administration – ordering and renewing, ensuring electronic access, payment, central split-invoicing and budget allocation
- access – special single-route, multi-site access for SwetsWise Online Content end-users
- training and support – ensuring maximum benefits from consortia deals.

The benefits to the LIS

The supplier in this case study claims a number of benefits for customer organizations. The primary benefit is in time saving, especially where the customer is a consortium; in this case the supplier provides some of the communication between consortium members. The supplier claims to understand the pressures faced by library and information professionals – from researchers who expect information to be freely available on the web, to the CEO who can't understand why it takes so long to negotiate enterprise-wide electronic access – and offers its experience to offset this. The services are delivered via a web browser interface, which enables individuals across your organization to order and manage subscriptions quickly and easily from their desktop, all within a centrally controlled approval process. Overall, the benefits of using an external service such as this can be summarized as follows:

- user-friendly interface
- complete online help facility supported by dedicated customer service staff
- budget control
- cost-efficient ordering – several approval and access levels
- various methods for end-user registration
- payment by credit card, invoice or p-card
- online reporting
- compatibility with e-procurement systems

- linking to e-journals
- customizable multilingual interface
- searchable online catalogue containing more than 260,000 titles.

Summary

In this chapter we have looked at some issues concerning the ownership of and rights in the use of information, and how the use of outsourcing agents can help. The case study has illustrated suppliers' claims that their products and services allow customers to devote their resources to more professional work than the management of subscriptions and other administrative tasks.

5

How to outsource

In this chapter we look at:

- drawing up the management plan
- selecting your supplier
- making the agreement
- licences and other documents
- the contract period
- copyright
- other areas that can be outsourced.

Scheduling the agreement

An outsourcing arrangement may have a deadline of some kind attached, for example, to take effect from the beginning of a particular financial or calendar year. Careful planning will be necessary to ensure that deadlines are not exceeded, with the consequent difficulties that would ensue. A scheduled plan, working backwards through the stages required, will provide the key dates for each stage of the process.

Table 5.1 lists the stages and times in the process of outsourcing all or most of a major library service; calendar dates may be assigned to each of the stages:

Table 5.1   Outsourcing schedule

Process	Time allocated	Start date of process
Contract starts	0 days	Contract date (Day C)
Contractor sets up on purchaser's premises	90 days	C–90 (3 months)
Contract signed	15 days	C–105
Final negotiations	15 days	C–120
Contract confirmed	5 days	C–125
Financial enquiries	30 days	C–155 *
Appeals	30 days	C–155 *
Contractor selected, unsuccessful shortlist candidates informed	10 days	C–165
Shortlist bids opened and evaluated	20 days	C–185
Shortlist invitations to tender issued	45 days	C–230 †
Appeals	30 days	C–230 †
Shortlist selected, unsuccessful longlist candidates informed	10 days	C–240
Longlist bids opened and evaluated	30 days	C–270
Longlist bids invited	30 days	C–300
Expressions of interest evaluated	20 days	C–320
Request for proposals issued	30 days	C–350
Advertisements placed	15 days	C–365
Decision to outsource	5 days	C–370

*   appeals against non-inclusion can be considered at the same time as financial enquiries are being made about the selected supplier (although clearly a successful appeal would either halt or lengthen the timetable).
†   appeals against shortlisting can be considered while the shortlisted suppliers are preparing their final bids, but again the decision to invite a further bid may lengthen the process.

Even without complications, Table 5.1 shows that it can take a consider-able time – a few days over a year in this example – to move from the decision to outsource a service to the point where a contractor is ready to take over. It is certainly possible to shorten this timetable, but there is increased risk to be evaluated at each stage in this case.

Table 5.1 shows both a longlist and a shortlist stage. You could move straight to a shortlist if the likely field is small – the expressions of inter-est will inform your decision. However, it costs a supplier money to submit a bid, whether successful or not, and the use of a longlist stage may give a wider range of suppliers the opportunity to submit an outline bid that can then be worked up in more detail by those invited onto the short-list. So, there is a balance to be struck between running an additional stage that could interest more suppliers, and running a single stage that will attract only those suppliers willing to invest time and money whether or not they are successful bidders.

You could reduce the time of handover to the contractor from three months, but this will depend on the complexity of the operation being outsourced, and it is better to find you have a few days in hand than have to make emergency arrangements when things are not ready in time.

Whatever level of risk you decide you are willing to accept on this timetable, you must convert it into a list of dates that correspond to the stages you are including in the outsourcing exercise. These dates should be included in documents issued to potential contractors and other inter-ested parties so there can be no doubt about contractual obligations.

A range of software is available to help with the planning process. Apart from the offerings from the major commercial software houses, there are less well known programs available through IT portal sites such as ZDNet (look under 'project management software' within 'business software').

The management plan needs to cover details such as who will take part in the evaluation meetings (taking care to check for holiday periods). Either as part of the plan or as a required outcome from the scheduled meet-ings, evaluation criteria should be produced based on the original service specification: these will allow the evaluation meetings to assess the quality of the bids against the requirements, and to ensure that the most important elements of the specification are given the highest weighting in the assessment.

Selecting your supplier

In practice, outsourced suppliers have been drawn from a range of organizations – some obvious, some not so obvious. If your outsourcing exercise is to be beyond reproach – which may mean beyond legal challenge in some circumstances –you need to be sure that you have identified all types of potential supplier and know how to reach them.

Among the types of supplier organization that might wish to bid are:

- specialist library and information consultancies
- specialist library materials suppliers
- facilities management companies
- other libraries, e.g. national libraries, other libraries in the sector, specialist libraries.

Suppliers can be identified from several sources. These include:

- the CILIP *Buyers' Guide*
- the news pages and advertisements in professional publications, e.g. *Library and Information Gazette, Information World Review*
- word of mouth – do not underestimate it
- published tender results such as contract award notices contained within the TED (*Tenders Electronic Daily*) database (http://ted.publications.eu.int), giving names and addresses of successful bidders.

The list of suppliers that you choose for your outsourcing project must be well chosen. You do not want to waste your time managing a tender process in which the suppliers do not bid because they are not interested in providing the category of services or supplies that you are seeking. So, ensure that the companies you choose are likely to be interested.

Your tender documents are likely to include requests for financial information, so unless it is very obvious that a company cannot manage financially – not a very likely event – you should leave judgements about the stability and backing of a supplier to your financial experts as part of the bid-evaluation process.

The bid evaluation is likely to be managed in line with your organization's rules on tendering and contracting, so a detailed description of one or other organization's methods is not really appropriate here. But here are some issues to keep in mind:

- How closely does the bid match what you specified? Has it met all the essential requirements, and how does it deal with desirable requirements?
- What weighting do you give to the various elements listed in the specification? In other words, would you give more weight to (say) a supplier who offers to provide and maintain a library computer installation with a two-hour maximum time to fix than to one who offers a four-hour time to fix? And, if so, how is that reflected in the weighting for the importance of cost?
- What has the supplier offered you that you weren't expecting? Is there, for example, an offer of free book servicing as well as a price discount?
- How much confidence do you have in the supplier's promises? Are there factors (like geographic location) that make you doubt that the service can be delivered as offered? Does the supplier say how these will be overcome? (It has been known for a supplier to say: 'We can't do what you want, but if you award us the business we'll set up a UK subsidiary to serve you'. This is a great promise, but how long would it take to put into effect and to be running well enough to provide the service quality required?)

You could set out these and other selection criteria in a table to help you. See, for example, Table 5.2.

Table 5.2 Evaluation of bid to supply a computer system

Bidder name	ABC suppliers			
Feature	Points	Weighting	Score	Comments
Essential requirements	7	3	21	Elegantly met
Desirable requirements	4	2	8	Several omitted
Confidence in supplier	8	2	16	Good reference sites
Additional features	7	1	7	Innovative ideas
TOTAL SCORE			52	

To use a table like Table 5.2, the bids are awarded points out of ten against each category, and these points are multiplied by the weighting before the scores are added to give a final mark. So, in this instance, and on the items shown, this supplier has achieved a score of 52 out of a possible 80. If there is no obvious winner then a more detailed evaluation must be carried out, looking at each category in turn to see whether any additional factors should be taken into account. Table 5.2 can be expanded for other relevant features, e.g. technical understanding or appropriately qualified staff, according to your requirements.

Remember to keep the table after the award so that you have evidence of the fairness of the selection process.

Making the agreement

Your agreement with the chosen supplier will be contractually binding, so it must be drawn up with the assistance of your legal and financial department. However, just because they are experts in their field do not let them put you off including features that suit your requirements. You can be sure that any library jargon will be cut out by the draft writer, and you must ensure that the resulting text expresses your requirements accurately. Further information on agreements is contained in Chapters 6, 7, 8 and 9.

In our work on service level agreements we have promoted the use of a glossary that defines library terminology in lay terms: then there can be no doubt about whether 'circulation' means sending round issues of the latest journals or issuing books on loan (both are valid meanings in library parlance), or whether the most rapid level of response to a help desk call is 'urgent', 'rush' or something else. This is particularly important where suppliers assign numbers to processes: for example, if the bid states that the supplier will allocate 'priority 1' status to calls from the library regarding equipment breakdowns, check how many levels of priority there are, whether priority 1 is higher or lower than priority 2, and whether there is a priority 0 that outranks it! Check whether the level of service available to you from your supplier differs at the weekend, especially if you offer Sunday opening.

When you are as happy as your legal and financial advisers you can agree to the documents being signed.

Copyright, licences and other documents

Make sure that your suppliers do not put you in a difficult position by failing to take out the necessary licences for the work they do on your behalf. Even if a breach of copyright turns out to be the supplier's legal liability, it will still reflect poorly on you if your supplier is summoned to court to answer to a software manufacturer or copyright collection society.

Be aware that there can be problems when an agent, such as an outsourcing supplier, subscribes to licensed content on your behalf: some content providers license only the organization that pays them. This means that in some circumstances your outsourcing supplier has the right to use materials but you do not. Word the relevant clause in your outsourcing agreement so that there is an option for you to obtain licences directly if the publisher's terms do not allow the onward disposal of rights that your supplier obtains, and so that the supplier is not penalized in these circumstances.

Consider all the forms of licensing that need to take place – copyright in books and periodicals, newspapers, broadcasts and educational materials, the use of cuttings, the reproduction of artistic works, and the use of electronic content, for example. Make sure that all are covered by the required current licences.

Consider what other documentation should be kept. There will probably be contractual documents recording the agreement or contract between the library and the supplier. Should a procedures manual be part of the documentation? It could record the system in place at the start of the contract, or form a constantly edited and updated manual that not only supports staff training and induction but records the agreed procedures against the possibility of the work returning in-house or a change of supplier.

Contract period

How long is right for an outsourcing contract? To some extent it depends on whether you are the purchaser or the supplier.

The supplier will want it to be as long as possible. This will allow the supplier to:

- predict income from the contract and reconcile this with the cost of running the service
- employ staff on a longer-term basis, bringing more stability to the contract and ensuring that the customer has a known contact for as long as possible
- use the income from the contract to increase profitability and (one would hope) to invest in developing the service and providing new facilitites.

The customer would like something shorter in duration, in order to:

- review the contract if the financial position changes drastically
- change supplier if service is poor, without waiting for the contract to end or taking legal action to enforce or sever the contract
- change to more innovative ways of delivering the service as they are developed and brought to market
- be flexible in buying only services that have active users.

In practice, some of these requirements can be met by careful drafting of the contract. If the agreement allows the two parties to agree a change in order to include new services or to exchange underused services for new ones, then there should be no problem and a win–win situation can be reached. If the contract is rigid, and perhaps runs for several years without any scheduled review meetings, then a less stable relationship is likely between the supplier and the purchasing library.

A one-year contract may be sufficient for small-scale operations, but it will not give staff a particularly long time to learn the library's business before they are exposed to the possibility of the contract being lost. This length of agreement is thus suited to short-term tasks or projects (e.g. catalogue conversion), or to tasks that do not require new staff to be trained to work within the organization (e.g. buying in additional generalist research services).

From the library's point of view a two- or three-year contract is probably best. It is long enough for the contractor's staff to get to know the subject and the clientele. It is short enough that, if a complete mistake has been made, the situation can be managed to minimize damage without the need to negotiate (and pay expensively for) the curtailment of a long contract. It is long enough to get to know whether a contractor has the ability to achieve an acceptable standard in the longer term (and thus whether an extended term can be awarded if this is within the contract terms, or else whether there is a good chance of re-awarding the contract if it is re-advertised).

A longer contract may be problematic if there are inadequate controls for review. In the event that the supplier's performance deteriorates during the first part of the contract (perhaps because the supplier has underestimated the effort needed) it would be difficult to negotiate a break in the agreement when the supplier has a financial incentive to keep it going. (The alternative of taking legal action over the declining quality could prove expensive and the case difficult to demonstrate.) There is also the question of whether a supplier could find itself the subject of a takeover during the lifetime of a longer contract, and whether the library would be comfortable dealing with the successor business. Again, careful wording of the contract might alleviate this potential problem.

Other services to outsource

Your organization, especially if it is a large public sector one, may well have other outsourcing agreements in place, so that things like building management and maintenance, transport and logistics, and perhaps even some professional services are supplied by external contractors. You may find you have no choice whether to use these services. But sights are being set wider than this. A number of major library projects now involve outsourcing the library building itself!

Outsourcing the building

The cost of building or extensively refurbishing a library building can be very high, as a number of library authorities have discovered. Here too outsourcing in one form or another can offer a solution to the problem. While, because of the complex issues of public funding, this is an area that is bounded by regulations far more extensive than this book can cover, it is worth looking for a moment at the methods libraries have adopted to tackle rebuilding or renovating their physical environment. Even small elements of some of the major projects mentioned here may provide ideas that solve local problems.

Two principal methods have emerged in the UK:

* co-location
* PFI and PPP – private finance initiatives and public–private partnerships.

Co-location

A very positive article about developments in Glasgow City Libraries (Hyams, 2002) notes that by co-locating community libraries in other facilities, not only are costs reduced but there are opportunities for proactive development of joint services and events. Glasgow's 1999 *Best Value Service Review* (Glasgow City Council, 1999) identifies two possible approaches, one a full-blown public–private partnership model (see below) that would provide the level of capital investment needed for its perceived requirements, the other an option for private sector involvement through tendered opportunities to 'develop, manage and make a commercial return' on opportunities such as shops and catering within premises managed by the Libraries and Archives Service. Elements of this second approach are increasingly visible in libraries even when a PFI or PPP approach is taken – for example with the letting of a coffee bar concession in the new Bournemouth library.

PFI and PPP – private finance initiatives and public–private partnerships

These two approaches involve essentially the same activity: the use of private sector capital to create a major public facility that includes both a library (gallery or museum) and revenue-generating activities such as hotels and shops on the same site. They have been used for both part and full funding of the capital outlay required for a major project. At the time of writing there are three major projects under way in the UK public library sector that are using this route – Bournemouth, Brighton and Haringey: the first two for new libraries, and the third for IT and facilities management support to a library and museum.

The outline business case for a PFI scheme in Newcastle was approved in late 2003 and is expected to lead to the refurbishment of three libraries within a year, and the construction of a new city library to open in 2007 (Newcastle City Council, 2003a, 2003b).

Of interest in this context is the approach made possible in France under a law of 1992. The new library that opened in March 2004, on the site of the former Alcazar music hall in Marseilles, qualifies for the status of Bibliothèque Municipale à Vocation Régionale (BMVR), meaning a municipal library that plays a specific role for the region, laid down by regulation. The Alcazar library not only meets the requirements of the municipality that supports it (it equals Paris's Pompidou Centre in physical space and the Sorbonne in the size – if not the content – of its collection), but it supports regional libraries that are therefore able to use its services rather than having to fund their own more advanced activities (Germain and Lorius, 2000). There is some resemblance to regional library collaboration in the UK and other countries, but the essential point here is that the presence and support of the larger library allow the smaller, community-based libraries to outsource some of their activities to the larger, publicly funded library. (The Marseilles project cost €61 million in total; this level of funding is unlikely to be on offer to small libraries.)

Summary

In this chapter we have looked at issues to do with the nature of outsourcing, and completed this with a look at some of the big ticket items that can be outsourced by libraries or their funding bodies. We looked at the timescale, and at the events that need to be scheduled. We examined ways to find suitable suppliers, and at the length of time that you might want agreements to last. And we noted that some organizations in the public sector in the UK and Europe are starting to take a very wide view of outsourcing, to the extent that the very fabric of the library can be provided and managed by an external supplier.

6

What to include in your outsourcing agreement

In this chapter we discuss:

- why we need agreements for outsourcing
- what is an agreement?
- the basic objectives of the outsourcing agreement
- keeping people in the picture
- what features can be included in the agreement?
- what agreements do not do
- negotiating and signing the agreement
- partial outsourcing
- managing multiple agreements
- monitoring the agreement.

Introduction

In recent years, service level agreements (SLAs) have become a common part of library and information service (LIS) activities. The debate continues as to whether an SLA will get in the way of providing a good service or enable the LIS to have more control over the types and levels of service provision. Looking at the more positive side, a number of benefits can be derived from having an agreement. All parties to the agreement including the users will have a better understanding of the services available, the quality of the services and the modes of delivery. If the LIS decides to outsource any of its services it will be necessary to have an agreement so that everyone understands what is involved, who is responsible for what and what exactly is expected from whom!

With that in mind, how can lessons from service level management be applied in managing outsourcing agreements?

The need for an outsourcing agreement

Whether you are outsourcing just one part of the service or the whole service, it is important to set out clearly the relationship between the supplier of the service(s) and the users. Both sides need a benchmark against which to test the efficiency and effectiveness of the services and products provided. The service provider needs to know the standards to which it must conform. Ultimately, service can be measured against these standards and, if that service is unsatisfactory, the agreement could be withdrawn and the functions retendered.

In an agreement, the supplier and users of services are clearly identified and develop an understanding of each other's requirements and abilities. A supplier is clearly accountable for the performance standards, quality and cost of its services, and any limitations or shortcomings.

On the other hand, users should clearly understand the cost of such services, and of any additional ones that may be required either within the existing agreement or in addition to it. The agreement should be such that users can monitor the volume and quality of services they are paying for, and the supplier can monitor its own capabilities and if necessary improve, by training, the staff offering the services. And at all times, both supplier and users should understand the mechanism for variation or termination of services.

What an agreement is
A contract

In effect, an outsourcing agreement is a contract because it is an agreement, usually between two parties, detailing the essential elements of services together with the timescales and performance levels to be provided by the supplier to the client. To that extent the agreement is binding and represents the goodwill of the parties, who have agreed on a level of services which both (or all) can sign up to, taking financial, staffing and other resources into account. Whether or not there are varying service levels for separate parts of the customer organization, the agreement says what the supplier is going to supply and what the customer agrees to accept. It should set out the way in which the service is going to be delivered, and what happens if it isn't. The supplier may choose to put this information into a statement of service or into a standard brochure and then refer to this in the agreement. It is entirely up to you as the customer whether to agree to this, but it has the advantage that if you refer to a standard published brochure there is less room for doubt in the unwelcome event of a dispute, since there will probably be many other potential reference sites that are using the same service.

Include a glossary

In specifying the services to be provided under an outsourcing agreement it is a useful exercise to have prepared a list of services which the LIS provides, including definitions as necessary. Even within a LIS there is considerable confusion over the multiple meanings of words such as 'circulation', 'series' and 'copy' and distinctions may well be lost if your generalist management staff put together a service specification without the benefit of professional advice. Contract managers may well rely on trade literature to guide their efforts: this literature is frequently of American origin and uses American terminology such as 'routing' and the American sense of terms such as 'circulation'. If you want to buy in journal circulation make sure that the specification says so; if your organization needs book circulation in the sense of the old-fashioned circulating library, say that. A moment's reflection will show that the document in question moves quite differently in each case, and its transits to and from the LIS are far greater in the second instance than the first. If it is necessary to draw out a distinction between 'circulation' (where the items circulated return to the LIS) and 'distribution' (where the users retain the documents sent to them), then draw that distinction in a glossary that you share with the potential bidders for the service. Precision in such matters at the outset will save considerable problems during the performance of the agreement.

Basic objectives of the outsourcing agreement

The basic objectives of an outsourcing agreement are to:

- state what the customer needs by providing a service statement
- show the mechanics and processes of fulfilling those needs
- describe the quantities of work to be handled and the ways of measuring them.

In doing this it:

- records what the purchaser wishes to buy and therefore what the supplier is expected to provide
- describes the agreed services in such a way that it is precise enough to act as an agreement but not so prescriptive that it prevents service development or precludes negotiated change to improve service.

Keeping people in the picture

It is essential that all levels of staff are consulted during the implementation of the agreement, because everyone's understanding of the levels of services to be achieved and the timescales within which these levels of services are to be achieved are implicit in the agreement. People within your organization will depend on the outsourcer to support them in achieving their own specified levels of performance within the business planning process, and the time to discover that there are problems with the outsourcer is not during your staff appraisal exercise a year later. If your team's assessment depends on the outsourcer providing them with a certain level of timely service, then make sure that the team is happy with what has been specified before the contract is confirmed.

Staff at all levels need to know what the full implications of the agreement are. Often it is the staff working at the enquiry desk, the interlibrary loans section, the search service section, or the ordering section, etc. who have the most detailed knowledge of the systems which will have to meet any agreements. For instance, it is no good accepting an interlibrary loans service that states that an item can usually be delivered within 48 hours when you know the norm is more like four days; the relevant expert member of your staff should be encouraged to challenge claims that are unlikely to be delivered in practice and ask how they are going to be achieved.

Features to include

Service agreements can be used to manage multiple relations with a number of players. They are often a feature of quality management systems where their precision aids the process of definition of products and services. They clarify the relationship between the supplier and the customer by setting out expectations and responsibilities, and the commitment of both parties to the agreement. Setting out the customer's responsibilities in the contract as well as the supplier's should avoid any arguments which can arise unnecessarily, for example where the customer has more details about a requested document than they actually reveal. The implied suggestion is that it is up to the supplier to find the item required with no further clues. And the agreement is a planning tool for the supplier, by allowing prediction of troughs and peaks of activity. In the outsourcing context, the terms that the potential supplier proposes for dealing with this situation should be reflected in your internal agreements – if your customers do not (or are not obliged to) tell you what they know about the more obscure publications or other information sources they want then you cannot provide the supplier with information.

Outsourcing agreements are prescriptive, but properly they should prescribe what is to be done rather than the manner of doing it. There are often alternative and possibly better ways of achieving the end which the external supplier may be freer to implement than the in-house supplier (e.g. by having a wider choice of ways to run software than the customer has on an internal IT system).

Any agreement should include details of exceptions – particularly anticipated and permissible exceptions – to the agreement. If a standard service is provided (which may be defined in a brochure or service statement) then the agreement need only refer to the standard terms and then list the variations, exceptions or enhancements.

The agreement will contain elements of a number of different types of specification in a single document. These include:

- Functional specification: a definition of what the system has to achieve or do, probably expressed in terms of outputs or achievements.
- Performance specification: setting levels of performance, for example by setting a minimum quota of actions to be completed in a stated time for various LIS functions (90% of enquiries from the management floor to be answered within 60 minutes).
- Technical specification: although it is to be avoided so far as possible, in practical terms it is probably not possible in many library and information services to exclude a definition of some of the systems and services to be used (The LIS will use the XYZ Ltd connection to Internet Services Providers Ltd for external electronic mail communications).

What agreements do not do

Agreements with outsourced suppliers need not be restrictive, but they can be and have been in practice when too little imagination is used and consequently the agreed terms allow no freedom to develop.

New models of service delivery can be established alongside the agreement: they have often proved to be necessary to fill in areas missed in the service definition, and partnerships have been set up with external suppliers to develop additional services or to provide investment in new areas. It is sometimes difficult to set up accounting systems that have the level of flexibility that the parties to an agreement might want to allow them to develop new services with a reasonable return on investment.

It is important to do your learning in a safe environment where you will not have to live with the results of any mistakes for several years to come. If there are likely to be problems with the team's acceptance of the use of agreements or contracts with your suppliers then resolve the issues before you go fully public. Similarly, you should work out what management and other information you want, and include that in your requirement. Remember that an outsourced supplier is likely to have a number of customers, so you may have to bargain strongly for additional information that other clients have not asked for. The payoff is that you can expect to be offered the results of work for other clients where the outsourcer believes it can sell on products developed to meet the wishes of particular clients.

Negotiating and signing the agreement
Client and supplier roles

The actual negotiation and signing of the agreement raises a number of issues. These issues are clarified first by looking at the client and supplier roles. A senior representative of the supplier will sign the agreement, while from the client side a senior member of the library management or the management board might be the signatory. If you use service level agreements internally, consider the relationship between the signatories to that agreement and those on the outsourcing agreement. If the client signatory for purchasing from an outsourcer is the same person as the supplier signatory on an SLA, he or she has a strong vested interest in getting the agreements to work. But there could be problems if the client signatory to the outsourcing agreement is considerably more senior than the supplier signatory on an internal agreement, since it may then be difficult to get the outsourcing manager to press the external supplier to improve. The outsourcing manager has to be persuaded that there is something in the arrangement for him or her too.

Contract management and staff performance

So you also need to think about how closely you bind together contract management and staff performance management. Is it proper for appraisal of the outsourcing manager to be directly linked to the reporting systems that monitor the performance of the contract? It is quite possible for the LIS manager to perform at a high level of skill and efficiency while at the same time the contract governed by the agreement is failing – and ask yourself whether you would consider it a failure of the contract manager's performance if the outsourced supplier failed because of the actions of another of its customers. We suggest that there should be the clearest possible separation of the two issues, although in practice it may be difficult to achieve total separation in a small organization or where there is a narrow management structure. It may be necessary to provide suitable training for procurement staff in order to allow them to report on contract performance in other business commands within the organization.

Management of disputes

How do you propose managing disputes in the contract relationship? Think carefully about how you involve your senior staff in the process, and how they will back up the outsourcing manager in your own team. It may be necessary to dissuade board members from placing themselves in this difficult position through excessive desire to be involved in the agreement management, especially if outsourcing services is a high-profile new activity that they want to be seen to take part in. And, while many issues can be settled amicably and informally, it is as well if senior managers do not start to form a cosy high-level management tier that may make it difficult to take serious decisions – contract management is undermined by informal agreements between senior managers. The ideal is for any disputes with suppliers to be settled at a lower level, leaving the most senior manager available in case of appeal or to provide final settlement of an evenly balanced argument.

The in-house team as potential supplier

There are complications if the LIS management team is also in the frame as a potential supplier, for example where contracting out is one possibility but the in-house team is invited to bid. Propriety demands that the team is excluded from the group of people defining the service requirement, but this is likely to cause problems in reaching an accurate specification since the LIS team consists of the only people likely to be able to write an accurate service specification. If there is a possibility of your service being put out to competition at a future date, it is as well to have a published and full statement of library and information services available well in advance of any competition. Otherwise, it would be reasonable to insist that the client side engages a consultant with LIS experience who is, preferably, acceptable to both client and supplier teams.

Partial outsourcing

Outsourcing may take place for only a part of the service. For example, in some organizations value added services (enquiries, selective dissemination of information (SDI), loans, online services) have been retained by the existing LIS while publications supply has been outsourced. Where direct purchasing organizations have been set up for local authority and other library and information services a similar approach has taken place. In these cases the LIS needs to make clear which services it provides and which are provided by an external contractor, and to set out the conditions of use that are imposed by the various providers. It would also be a good time to set out any constraints on the service, for example if you are using consolidation services for your journals supply to publicize the likely delay (which may be in hours rather than days) between the arrival of subscription copies sent direct to members of the organization and the library copies, which will need some processing and may have to be further shipped from the outsourcer's premises to your offices. This extends to the use of external contractors for parts of the work of the LIS such as indexing, or updating loose-leaf publications. Do you, for example, need to issue details of the times of visits by the loose-leaf filing service, or ask that people make their offices available for the filer to work in at the time of the visit? There will be some considerable communications work to do on these issues, particularly if this is a service that has previously been part of the LIS. You need to explain about the new people who appear in offices to do work that was previously done by the in-house LIS team. You need to reassure people that, if they deal with your supplier's help desk in future when chasing missing journals, this does not mean that you are any the less concerned about the quality of the service. There is more about communications in Chapter 12.

The agreement will clearly need to specify some other details such as the starting date, conditions for payment where this applies, and any conditions concerning equipment or other services which must be used by the supplier. (This might, for example, prevent the LIS from changing to another computer system which it considers better than the existing one, or which is able to use electronic data interchange with a supplier.)

Managing multiple agreements

A variation on the offer of a part of the service for contracting out is the offer of multiple agreements. This situation may arise through the gradual introduction of outsourcing in a large organization, with the LIS making initial agreements for part of the service or for specified parts of the organization, with the intention of extending the arrangements throughout the community at a named later date. Care is needed to keep multiple agreements in line with one another or there is a risk of a two- or even three-tier service, with one group of customers getting a different level of service from others because of the differing suppliers, or differing specifications.

Monitoring the agreement

Chapter 9 is devoted to keeping the agreements on target and monitoring the service, and the detailed mechanisms are explored there. But it is important at the agreement drafting stage to ensure that monitoring systems are built in; and that both sides are committed to them not as an inconvenience but as a basis for discussion and understanding

Summary

An ideal outsourcing agreement should resemble an internal service level agreement and should be maintained in line with any such SLAs. It should comprise:

- a short covering contract document, to which is appended
- a detailed specification with annexes containing other information and amendments.

The essential elements of the covering contract document include:

- a brief general statement summarizing the services to be provided (full details are in the specification or an accompanying brochure or guide)

- definitions of the two parties to the agreement, setting out who is providing the service (the supplier) to whom (the client)
- a statement of the duration of the contract.

The document will contain other important specific information such as dependencies on related agreements, and will include details such as the monitoring arrangements and the conditions under which either party can request (or demand) amendments to or termination of the agreement.

7

Elements of the outsourcing agreement

In this chapter we consider:

- who the agreement is between and how the roles are defined
- what elements you need to put into the agreement
- working with procurement specialists.

Introduction

Just as with other contracts and service level agreements, it is vital that the details are right or you will be faced with ongoing problems once the outsourcing agreement goes into effect. The specification of the service is especially important and it will require work by the purchaser with and without the supplier to ensure that the documents show exactly what the purchaser's expectations are.

As we shall see, some of the usual rules may need to be suspended. If your procurement professionals insist on writing the documents, then you must make sure that they understand enough of your business to be able to specify accurately what you want and not what they think you mean. If the information service as a whole is being outsourced, it can also happen that, in order to avoid accusations of distorting the tender process, the professional staff will not be consulted over the definition of the service's role.

Other rules become more important. For example, service delivery measurements must be well defined, because quantity of service delivered does not necessarily have any bearing on quality delivery. (You can produce large volumes of catalogue records in a short time, but that does not prove that they are any use in tracking the library's collection.)

Who the agreement is between

This may not be an entirely straightforward issue. In some organizations contracts are let centrally so that the agreement is not made directly between the library and the supplier but between the organization's contracts or procurement department and the supplier. This can lead to some problems – you may find that you are spending time educating your contracts team to understand the business that both you and the supplier are fully conversant with. However, there is usually little that you can do about this, other than patiently explaining to the contracts team why particular issues matter so much, and you have the advantage of knowing that contractual issues are properly taken care of.

Defining the roles

The aim of any contract should be clarity, so it is sensible to make sure that your outsourcing agreement or agreements set out clearly the roles to be played by each partner. It is obvious enough that one party is the supplier and the other is the consumer or purchaser of that supply, but it is helpful to state where the dividing lines fall and, if possible, to assign names to roles so that all parties know who is doing what. Who is the manager on each side who should make the initial contact on contract management issues, on library management issues, or to report an operational problem? Whose responsibility is it to check that bibliographic data are correct for ordered publications – the library or the supplier? Who ensures that technical systems are operating properly?

Elements in the agreement

What other elements might be included in an outsourcing contract? They could be any or all of the following:

A general preamble

This describes the situation at the point where the contract is let, naming the library or its parent body as the organization that wishes to reach an agreement for the provision of library services. Where only part of the service is being outsourced, the preamble should state this early on.

A statement of the services

This must be provided in as much detail as is necessary to avoid doubt or ambiguity, while at the same time not over-specifying to the point that any opportunity for initiative or development is lost.

Conditions of contract

These are likely to be added by your procurement and legal people, but you should consider carefully what elements you require in the document if they do not already appear.

Taxes

What is the position on payment of value added and other taxes? Library and information services pay VAT on databases and other services, but books and periodicals remain exempt in the UK. Some subscriptions are not taxed at the full rate because they are deemed to contain non-taxable elements such as member publications alongside chargeable services. Will the supplier charge the full rate of tax on the package provided, and are your financial advisers content that this is the true position? Clearly each case will vary, but it will be helpful to check the position before signing a contract in order to ensure that your library is not going to pay over the odds, and also that you are not creating a nightmare for your finance department!

Handling disputes

Even in the best run contract a dispute might arise over a misunderstanding. Disputes are destructive when they are unresolved or leave one party feeling hurt by the outcome. If this happens it is the worst time to discover that the contract says nothing about who should be involved in settling the dispute, or where the parties go for arbitration and decision if they cannot agree. Make sure that the contract is fair to both parties but does not give scope for protracted stalemates; it could set time limits before the parties must escalate the dispute to higher levels of management, or must together seek arbitration if settlement is not reached.

Default

What happens if you outsource an operation to a company that then defaults, either because it cannot manage to do what it has contracted or, worse, because it goes into administration or receivership and is unable to continue? You should aim to include an element in the contract that will avoid your service being brought to a halt because you are locked into a supplier who is unable to deliver. You must define the trigger point that will bring these provisions into effect, such as the failure to deliver any ordered publications for 14 or 28 days, or the placing into receivership of the supplier's business. Advice from your legal advisers is essential, and you may rest assured that the legal department of potential suppliers will go through your requirements very thoroughly, so ensure that you ask for what is important to you rather than what you would quite like or think you might just get away with. We look further at this issue in Chapter 9.

Duty of care

You need a guarantee that your supplier will act in your best interests and will take just as much care as you would if you were continuing to run the services directly. A section stipulating that the supplier has a duty of care can be reinforced by statements setting out how this is to be done, such as insisting that all reference enquiries are verified from two sources before being considered authentic, and that customers are warned when it has not been possible to corroborate an item of information from a second source.

You must also insist that your supplier applies the same standards of service that you would when dealing with third-party suppliers. The Fargo Public Library in the USA was recently reported to have severed its contract with its management contractor because subscriptions had become overdue and lapsed – including, ironically, the subscription to the local newspaper that reported the problem (Breaking News, 2003). It was established that a few bills had been delayed for up to six weeks, resulting in the loss of continuous subscriptions to the items concerned. Although the remainder of the contract was operating satisfactorily and it had recently been extended for two years, the public library's board decided that this was sufficient reason to cancel the remainder of the contract.

Hours of work

These need to be carefully set out in any contract, as do the days on which that work takes place. This item has been complicated in recent years by the trend to longer weekend opening of public libraries, so that you may be looking for a supplier capable of a seven-day operation. In the university and business sectors this may be a 24-hour operation. In a few cases it may be a requirement for the supplier to work unusual or long hours and to collaborate with suppliers to the organization's offices in other countries. Hours need to be carefully defined, as does the level of service available at each time and location.

Access to and occupation of premises

The supplier must be given rights to enter and occupy the appropriate areas of your premises, even if there has been agreement that services will be delivered from a remote site. The supplier must also be able to meet customers to discuss information needs, and this is better done by direct meeting than by telephone, e-mail or self-fill questionnaire without personal help from an information team member. In many organizations security is now of paramount importance, so that adding this statement to the service specification will emphasize the importance of having the supplier's staff cleared to enter the premises.

Facilities provided

The supplier needs to know exactly what is supplied and what it will either have to provide for itself or will be charged for:

- Apart from the usual requirements for suitable serviced office space, can the supplier expect unlimited telephone service (dial-up, ISDN or Broadband?) and access to the computer network?

- Which networks does the internal network connect to, for example an extranet linking to partner companies or other stakeholders?

- Are there limitations on the software that can be run (such as Flash or streaming media) and does the network impose any limitations on the services that can be provided (e.g. because it uses dynamic IP addressing and special arrangements must be made with electronic journal providers)?

- Will services such as internal directories be provided and will the supplier's personnel be listed there?
- What internal facilities are available (this might include sports and social facilities as well as work-related services)?

Technical clauses

You may want to provide potential suppliers with information about the networks and systems with which they will be working. For example, if you are specifying that the supplier should or may use application service provider (ASP) technology to deliver a library housekeeping system via the internet using a browser, you could usefully include details of the current browser software (program and version) on your system as well as details of the operating system and available bandwidth for connection to the internet. The supplier will not assume that you have a Windows-based system and needs to know what you operate, especially if your organization has gone for open source (such as Linux) or runs unusual versions of the operating system.

Relationships with other parties

A statement of a requirement for the library to maintain membership of co-operative schemes or other interlibrary organizations will remind the supplier that negotiation with third parties is necessary. You will need to include statements about legal obligations such as the handling of personal data under the Data Protection Act, which will also highlight areas needing particular attention, and remind suppliers that they need to satisfy you that their procedures will shield you from legal challenge. If the supplier is known to handle information outside the European Union (for example, in order to rekey catalogue card data, which contain personal information) then care should be taken to include a suitable requirement in the agreement.

Duration of contract

A statement about the duration of the agreement is highly recommended. This works in two ways. It gives the client the right to terminate the agreement early, but its main purpose is to set out the contract's expected length, which should probably be three or five years. A second clause gives the option to extend a successful agreement without the need to go to the expense and inconvenience of a new tender operation. The option date should give at least six months' notice.

Transfer of responsibility

The contract should have clauses about the transfer of responsibility should the supplier wish to transfer the work to another organization. This will protect the LIS interests. If a different organization is required to take on the service at the expiry or termination of the agreement, the LIS should co-operate in the transfer. The transfer should be arranged to achieve the minimum interruption in the services.

Working with procurement specialists

If you work in any kind of large organization there is likely to be a specialist team whose job is to manage procurement and purchasing. You will probably need to work with them to ensure that your organization's rules on purchasing are observed, and that you do not end up in breach of any financial or accounting rules. The value of subscriptions has risen to such a point that the budget of even a medium-sized library, if spent with a single supplier, is likely to exceed the limits that exempt small contracts from being tendered through European Commission and General Agreement on Tariffs and Trade (GATT) procedures in European countries, so you may well need support in placing notices in the *Official Journal* and in managing a tender exercise to select your supplier.

If there is an official purchasing specialist whose services are available to you at little or no cost, then make good use of that person rather than taking a risk and putting yourself in breach of the law. The downside of this arrangement is that you must ensure that your specialists understand your business, and do not put unnecessary obstacles in the way. A particular sticking point may be in explaining how the purchase of information services varies from purchasing bulk items such as stationery: each published item is sufficiently unique that alternatives will not do (when your usual brand of paper clip is sold out, you can usually find an alternative to hold your papers together, but a chemistry textbook is not the best substitute for Catherine Cookson); you often cannot tell how much of a service you will want to purchase at any given time (e.g. how many minutes you will need to search on *Chemical Abstracts* next March). Add to this the complication that, although there are different suppliers from whom you can purchase, there is only one publisher of a given title (unlike the many makers of similar paper or pens) and you can perhaps see why some purchasing professionals think that the library and information world is a little too specialist for general solutions to apply.

Whatever the case in your own organization, ensure that you not only stay within the rules but make the most use of the help on offer so you do not need to spend your own professional time learning how to do another professional's job.

Summary

In this chapter we have looked at a number of the elements of outsourcing agreements and the issues that library and information professionals need to be thinking about when contracts are being drawn up.

We have identified several areas where it would be wrong to assume that standard contract clauses will cover the eventualities that the LIS is likely to encounter. And we have stressed that you must take sufficient heed of the advice of other specialists who may work in your organization and who can help you to put together a well written agreement; at the same time you must ensure that they do not ignore your need for accuracy on the LIS specialist issues in order to give themselves an easier life!

8

What the outsourcing agreement should look like

In this chapter you will find:

- a model format for the agreement document
- sample descriptions of services
- sample statements of service availability
- sample statements covering delivery of LIS materials and services.

Model format of the agreement document

Having decided to outsource a particular service or services you must ensure that all aspects of delivery are covered in your agreement. In the previous chapter we looked at the general conditions of contract and other prefatory material to include in your agreement. In this chapter we look at questions more closely related to the LIS, and suggest a model format for the agreement with a commentary on each section. Your local circumstances will affect the elements you include and the exact wording you choose.

The agreement document should contain, in the introduction, a statement of the format of the document. In this way, you and your customers, the receivers of the service, know exactly what to find. We suggest the following format:

- conditions and definitions for the agreement
- general description of the services available from the LIS and the outsourced service or services to be provided by the contractor
- a schedule of the services from within that general description that the agreement provides to the customer group or division in an organization
- definitions or glossary of terms used in the document
- annexes giving details of, for example, general conditions of the contract; help desks or contact name, telephone numbers etc.; schedules of additional sources agreed with the customer; or services to the public
- change control procedures etc., giving the date of the document.

Sample descriptions of services

In this section we suggest the elements to include in a statement of the range of services that may or may not be outsourced. Customers will select from the range, so this list should be comprehensive and leave no doubts in the customer's mind exactly what the outsourced service is providing. The following general information and basic details might be used for a special LIS. They could be adapted for academic or public use, while public librarians (and others) can also draw usefully upon the model standards document (1995) drawn up by The Library Association (now CILIP).

Delivery points

Location details of the information centre or LIS should be stated, so that it is clear which operations are covered by the agreement. If these locations are listed and identified in the organization's internal directory, refer to this; otherwise they will need to be set out in the document. Listing these in an annexe reduces change control problems, and allows any alterations to locations to be published as an internal notice.

If there are any restrictions on the use of particular libraries (e.g. a legal collection, which may be reserved for, or where first call is given to, lawyers), this is the place to include that information.

Now there is an increase in home working, consideration needs to be given to what exactly constitutes a 'delivery point'. It may be that, because of the type of work carried out by the end-user, research, access to data-bases, and SDI services will be used more by the individual user who is physically located outside the organization rather than by a section within it, so provision for this type of access must be included in the agreement.

Standard library and information services

Here you will need to state quite firmly what are considered to be the basic, or standard, services. A typical statement would be:

> Answering enquiries on all subjects of interest to organization XYZ based on collections of publications held as reference material and/or for lending at the main LIS and branch libraries, and using external sources to support these collections.

Here you could include a statement of what the LIS provides (a mission statement or statement of purpose), for example:

> The XYZ LIS provides and promotes an information and loans service that informs and supports the work of organization XYZ.
> The LIS also provides an enquiry service on XYZ organizational matters for members of the public, as described in paragraph 0.0 and subsequent references from that paragraph.

Also state here if the LIS provides professional support and facilities to other linked organizations, for example, to other companies within the group or to associated charities, or in support of other local authority serv-ices.

Current awareness service

When a current awareness service is provided, based on the regular pro-duction and circulation of a list of recently acquired LIS materials likely to be of interest to customers (e.g. based on the organization's interests or reflecting the interests of divisions in a given building), a description should be inserted. For example:

> Availability: is this available organization-wide, or to particular divisions or departments?
> Format: is a paper copy available to certain groups of users only, with others having to use a bulletin board or receive e-mail copies?
> Frequency: state the frequency and time of publication and note any exceptions (e.g. at public holiday times).

A statement can be also be made about available related and complemen-tary internal or external services.

Loan of LIS material

Describe the service of lending documents from the LIS stock to cus-tomers in the organization for pre-set and notified durations of time.

If different time periods apply to different groups (e.g. faculty, senior management), these should be detailed here. Put the details in an annexe to avoid the need for frequent change control for the main document:

> The loan periods are set out in Annexe A and may be varied by three months' notice to the LIS committee. LIS materials not required by another reader may be renewed but must be produced for checking at every fourth renewal.

Document supply

The terminology used by an LIS varies considerably and the definition of a 'document' used by your LIS may be wider than that used here. You must include a statement that makes clear the terms on which documents are supplied. It should be made particularly obvious that the LIS operates only on these terms, so that accepting a document supplied by the LIS binds the user to respect the intellectual property rights in it: copyright for printed materials, and performing and other rights in videos, software and multimedia items. For example:

> 'Document supply' means the supply of photocopies of extracts from documents in the LIS stock, regulated by the provisions of the law of copyright, and the additional provisions of the licence from the Copyright Licensing Agency held by the LIS. Alternatively, it means the supply of extracts from documents held in remote databases by commercial and other suppliers, and regulated by agreements in force concerning the copyright in those documents.

Consider the implications of more full text being available directly to the end-user. The LIS must ensure that the data are copyright cleared before offering such services. (See Pantry and Griffiths, 2002.)

Information retrieval

Many users are probably unaware that you obtain material from remote databases. If there is a company policy about connection to external services, this is where it should be picked up, for example:

> The retrieval and presentation of selected records taken from remote computer-held databases of information, or from databases on CD-ROM held in the LIS. Unless otherwise specified in Annexe B, searches are carried out in the LIS by information staff using details provided by the customer.

Selective dissemination of information

Many library and information services offer SDI services of one form or another; these may vary from one customer group to another. The service should be defined, together with any riders identifying services restricted to certain groups of users. If these restrictions are for the duration of the agreement, they are inserted here; if they change, or are likely to change, they should be detailed in an annexe. For example:

> A service providing current information from the LIS database(s), or from external databases, to selected customers or groups of customers in the departments, by matching the indexing terms of newly published materials with the search profiles of customers.

Interlibrary loans

These may be defined as:

> Loans of material borrowed from elsewhere, arranged through the XYZ LIS for its customers.

You may wish to add a note about any limits on the number of loans per section or per person at any one time. You should ensure that your users are aware of the restrictions that apply to you, and insist that they return loaned items on time. You may need to explain that it is irrelevant whether the loan has been arranged by your staff or by the outsourced supplier: the important point is that the conditions of use have to be observed for the benefit of all users, and it is the users who suffer from delinquent behaviour among their number, not the supplier. If there are problems with the supplier, there are proper channels to handle this; 'punishing' the supplier by misuse of the service is not a sensible reaction.

Purchase of publications

An LIS may act as the intelligent purchaser of publications across the organization, not just for its own stock. This wording defines this service, and adds some restrictions to make it clear that the LIS retains control of the budget. You may wish to consider some extra details if your budget is limited from the outset, or if you have a budget to spend on behalf of other divisions in an organization:

> The purchase and provision for use within organization XYZ of documents specified by customers for purposes that make the provision of a loan copy or copies inappropriate, but subject to any restrictions on supply brought about by the LIS budgetary management, and otherwise at the discretion of the LIS. The LIS may instruct the outsourced supplier not to act on direct instructions from customers to purchase publications.

Abstracting

In organizations such as research bodies, the LIS may write abstracts of the literature entering the organization and add this to an LIS or organization-wide database. This definition may also be useful if the research teams compile abstracts as part of their work and expect income from the abstracts when used by the rest of the organization:

> Making and recording on the LIS database a summary of the information in a document that has been catalogued and/or indexed in the LIS.

You could consider whether you need to include a clause making it clear that any commitment or agreement with the existing LIS to provide indexing and abstracting from circulated journals is carried across to the outsourced supplier's benefit.

Cataloguing

A definition of cataloguing is useful not only for the work done by the LIS but also when separate records are created that relate to a special collection. The standards should preferably be universally recognized. Typically, the Anglo-American Cataloguing Rules (AACR2) should be used, at a stated level of detail within the Rules, but otherwise there should be a defined and measurable standard against which compliance can be examined:

> The creation of bibliographic records according to stated and agreed standards and their incorporation into the LIS database.

Indexing

In a similar way, indexing standards must be established within the agreement. It may be necessary, in the schedule or in an annexe, to state whose responsibility it is to provide the thesaurus used. Clearly, there is a wide difference in start-up costs between running off a further copy of an in-house thesaurus, or providing access to its database, and that of purchasing a set of Library of Congress subject headings. The standards may be defined as:

> The creation or enhancement of bibliographic records with terms from the indexing language listed in the LIS thesaurus [or other agreed sources] in order to allow their later retrieval for current awareness or in response to enquiries.

Circulation of periodicals (circulation management)

Many library and information services circulate periodicals within the organization. The restrictions or conditions on this service can be set out in detail in the agreement, and any lists of titles should go in an annexe:

> The distribution by the supplier through [internal] mail services of consecutive issues of periodicals to users named in sequence on a list compiled from requests to view copies on circulation which have been agreed by the XYZ LIS.

With the availability of the electronic journal the LIS must ensure that only those with agreed access should be allowed the password to e-journals. It may be that the agreement is for all the organization to have access to a set of e-journals. The LIS will need to ensure that the agreement with the e-journal supplier reflects this. Bear in mind the variations in costs. For example:

> Access to an agreed range of e-journals will be arranged through the LIS including the table of contents, full text and archive.

Include any restrictions here, such as only allowing full-text access to certain users. The LIS must ascertain from the user group if it needs access to electronically held archives of journals. The LIS may have decided that the print holdings with the LIS should satisfy the users, but if arrangements are to be made with suppliers for electronic access to archive files then this should be part of the agreement with them:

> Access to agreed e-journals; archives for named users will be arranged through the LIS.

Binding

Some library and information services provide access to a binding service, which in most cases has been provided by external specialist suppliers for many years. The exact wording in the agreement will of course reflect the work done (e.g. collation, minor repair work, etc.):

The LIS [or the outsourced supplier] will prepare loose publications and other material owned by the organization and undertake binding or rebinding as required [or binding or rebinding will be undertaken by a chosen external contractor].

Disposal of publications

The LIS should have the right to dispose of documents that it no longer requires, to prevent wastage in terms of storage costs and staff time involved in maintenance. It may be necessary to include further defining text, for example if the LIS holds material as part of a co-operative, particularly where this entails holding items that would otherwise be judged fit for disposal.

You must consider carefully whether to pass these rights to an outsourced contractor; and, if you do, ensure that all obligations to retain material are explicitly set out in the agreement documents.

Advisory services

A statement defining professional advisory services can be useful, not least as a means of advertising the skills of the LIS staff beyond the purely custodial role that many observers believe to be the limit of their value. For example:

Advice to the organization's departments on [for example, the indexing of publications, and the organization and classification of collections of publications or of other information resources held within departments . . .]

Can the outsourcer provide any additional advice that your staff are not equipped to offer? This may be somewhat difficult to admit, but look at what is available and whether it could benefit your customers.

Copyright advice

It takes training and constant updating to answer or obtain answers to copyright queries from both within the organization and from the public. A reference to the Copyright Acts and related secondary legislation may be required here. The reference to LIS privileges establishes further reason for the LIS to lay claim to this area of work; check with your advisers that your agreement with the outsourcer maintains these privileges. For example:

> The LIS will advise the organization's departments on aspects of copying from published sources and on LIS privileges. It will also administer the photocopying licences to the organization from the Copyright Licensing Agency, the Newspaper Licensing Agency and the Ordnance Survey, and provide advice to departments on licensed copying. The LIS will administer a system for multiple copying from copyright materials.

Include a reference too 'taking further legal or other advice as required, and seeking advice on Crown copyright' – i.e. an acknowledgement that Crown and Parliamentary copyrights are difficult areas where the LIS may need standing agreement to incur expenses by seeking professional legal advice, consulting government departments or contacting the residual HMSO in order to give proper advice. Once again, consider whether you want to give the outsourcer these rights or retain them, especially if you think your legal advice is cheaper or better than theirs.

Remember to make reference to your users' responsibility to observe copyright in materials provided from your LIS.

Sales of the organization's publications

This is a commonly outsourced function of the information service, and a number of suppliers act for major organizations to store and distribute publications to the public either free of charge or against payment. If you are the sales point for the organization, wording such as that below will define the role. If you do not want to pass this role to an outsourced supplier, it may still be appropriate to make the second reference to knowledge of the publishing output of the organization in your agreements, in order to establish the principle. For example

> Where specified in Annexe C to this agreement, the sales of and accounting for publications by the organization. To maintain a database of publications by organization XYZ and to provide details of these publications to callers/members of the public.

Additional information and LIS services

If you want the supplier to provide additional services, these need to be specified in the agreement with the appropriate level of detail. They may include database management, records and archive services, technical and computer management, or directory compilation.

In a public or academic LIS, other services will be offered, and the performance indicators proposed in the Department of National Heritage's consultation paper *Reading the Future* (DNH, 1997) include accounting for issues of audiocassettes (music and spoken word), CD-ROMs and computer software, so definitions of these services may well be required, with supporting statements of availability and service standards placed later in the document. Online and electronic media are also proposed as access and usage categories, so the detail suggested here may need to be further developed.

Sample statements of service availability

In this section we suggest clauses that set the description of services into a local context: when and where the service will be available, the activities at each of the locations used by the LIS, and some statements of times at which the service will be unavailable, whether by design or because of some other conditions that make the LIS unavailable or unusable for some reason. A priority, where a service level agreement also exists, must be to ensure that, if the LIS is out of action through a situation beyond its control, it cannot be held to be in breach of its agreements. For example:

> LIS services will normally be available Monday to Friday from 09.15 to 17.30 [or whatever days of the week and times are agreed], or, in branch LIS, at such other times as displayed or agreed with customers and recorded in Annexe D to this agreement. The service point may, at the discretion of the head of the LIS or other officer in charge, pass the enquiry (request, etc.) to another service point [or to the contracted external provider] for completion.
>
> Services may be available outside these hours either by telephone or personal call to other LIS service points. Telephone numbers are listed in Annexe E to this agreement and are shown on the LIS publicity materials.
>
> Services will be curtailed or suspended on the occurrence of one or more of the following events:
>
> (a) any breakdown in building facilities and utilities (including computer systems, whether or not maintained by LIS) making it impossible to access information services
>
> (b) suspension or curtailment of public transport services affecting the area
>
> (c) any trades dispute affecting LIS staff or service provided to the LIS, including those affecting originators, providers, carriers or deliverers of information and documents
>
> (d) any breakdown in building facilities and utilities making it impossible to maintain safe, hygienic or tolerable working conditions within the terms of the Offices, Shops and Railway Premises Act 1963, the Health and Safety at Work etc. Act 1974, or any other relevant legislation from time to time in force

(e) public holidays, privilege holidays or other days on which the organization is otherwise closed for business

(f) closure or evacuation of the building, or part of the building occupied by the LIS or its stock.

In these cases apart from (e), best endeavours will be made to provide a service or to produce copies of documents from other sources, but no guarantee can be given. In cases of national or regional crisis or emergency, a weekend service may be provided by arrangement, but this agreement will be suspended for the duration of the supply of any such services.

You must ensure that this part of the agreement is constantly revisited and amended. Any new legislation affecting conditions in offices or other premises used by the LIS will have to be included. You might prefer to suspend service altogether if there is a major emergency.

You must consider whether to extend the wording to cover the location and premises of the outsourced supplier (and be ready to explain why you are interested in the current state of public transport in another part of the country entirely).

A report in the form shown below will be supplied at monthly intervals detailing any interruptions to the service lasting for more than two working hours as a result of any of the events listed in sections (a), (b), (c), (d) or (f) above.

You will already be supplying a considerable amount of information to your customer and this can quite easily be detailed on the form. With luck the monthly report will be routine, apart from the odd bank holiday and fire drill. However, this can be quite a serious point. When organizations and companies that observe different public holidays supply services to one another, some bizarre situations can arise. Organizations with offices in Scotland will find this a strong likelihood, because Scotland has different bank holidays from England, Wales and Northern Ireland, and some local holidays are observed in particular cities.

Case study

In one instance, the only workers in a building owned by organization C were the telephone operators supplied by supplier K, which observed a different additional day's holiday at Christmas. When organization C's employees returned to work, they found that the switchboard was unmanned, because the supplier had observed an extra day's holiday at New Year.

Consider the wording that allows for, or forbids, the locking or otherwise of the LIS at night, and for allowing your trusted customers the occasional use of reference books overnight. If the stock is outsourced, either because you have passed ownership of it to the supplier or because you made it a condition that the supplier provides the stock, whose responsibility is it if items of stock are stolen?

> Access to the LIS room(s) will normally be available outside the hours stated, but this is not guaranteed [or access to the LIS room is not available outside the hours stated except by special arrangement and appropriate payment to the contractor for overtime of its personnel]. LIS materials normally restricted to the LIS room(s) may exceptionally be provided on short-term loan in order to make them available outside the hours stated at the discretion of the head of the LIS or the officer in charge. [The replacement cost of any loss or damage to stock as a result of these arrangements shall be borne by organization XYZ or by the contractor, who shall demonstrate that adequate insurance is held.]

Sample statements of delivery of LIS materials and services

We now move to general statements regarding the delivery of services and documents to the customer. These statements relate to services provided to members of the organization, and can be adapted depending on the exact nature of the relationship between the external supplier and the LIS organization.

We talk about services to the general public later in this chapter (pages 103–4).

> At least one professional librarian information specialist shall normally (defined as during 98% of opening hours) be available at each service point during the hours listed in Annexe F. At other times professional staff may be provided at one or other LIS site.
>
> The supplier will use all its resources, both internal and external, to meet customers' requirements within the constraints of time, economy and staffing.
>
> Requests for access to published books, periodicals, reports, official publications, audiovisual materials, maps, standards, etc. ('publications') will be assessed by the LIS staff and copies provided for loan or retention, from stock, by purchase order, or by borrowing from other collections as appropriate. Requests may be made by telephone, in person, in writing or by electronic mail. Customers will provide such information as is available to assist the LIS staff and their suppliers in tracing correctly the bibliographic description and location of publications.

The next paragraph regulates the reuse of copyright material and could demonstrate the determination of the LIS to observe the law in the case of a discovered breach. It may need to be reinforced by a statement regarding fair dealing and any other areas of company or LIS policy on copying. Obviously, it will need to be amended in the light of the licences held. There was discussion of this issue in Chapter 5, and we look at communication aspects in Chapter 12. The paragraph might read:

> All LIS material supplied for use by customers is provided subject to the law of copyright and the terms of the licences to organization XYZ from the Copyright Licensing Agency, the Newspaper Licensing Agency and the Ordnance Survey, of Crown or parliamentary copyright, or of any more specific restrictions applying to other materials such as unpublished theses. Materials supplied to LIS customers may not be further copied or otherwise used outside the provisions of copyright law as extended by the licences held for organization XYZ.

Take care on this section and be sure that, if you describe licences held by your supplier, you have not either given away rights or set yourself up to infringe. You may wish to give your LIS an explicit right to use electronic services in the first instance; indeed, some suppliers look quite favourably on this approach.

You should now give a more general indication of the level of technical support and the systems capacity required (bandwidth and the maximum size of file that can be sent safely across the office network). Make a further statement about copyright, this time to insist that copyright notices and provenance tags in electronic records should not be removed; you should decide whether you want to place this obligation on the supplier, and you should impose it on your customer base. The paragraph might read:

> The LIS will use electronic information retrieval systems wherever appropriate or when significant savings in cost or effort appear possible. The results of such searches will be delivered by electronic mail wherever they are available in a form suitable for transmission by this means to a mailbox currently available to the customer. Files delivered in this way may not be further used other than for printing out. In

particular, they may not be stored in electronic form for further use with retrieval software unless a specific request for the required clearance has been made at the time of ordering and the head of the LIS has indicated that the appropriate fee has been paid. All copyright notices and other provenance markings attached to electronic files must be retained unaltered with the data to which they refer.

The following statement may need to be reinforced for senior management customers – and you may need to make it clear that failure is not a sacking offence, nor is it a valid reason to ring the supplier and shout:

When there is a deadline, every effort will be made to meet it.

You will, however, still need to give yourself some leeway:

The supplier will endeavour to provide services as quickly as possible. Answering machines may be used to provide a telephone service at busy times but in this case recorded requests will be answered or acknowledged within two working hours or if possible any shorter deadline stated by the customer.

You must include a statement about the accuracy of information retrieved, whether online or in print. It can be used to ensure that new editions of reference works are purchased, or that databases with an acceptable frequency of updating are used. Exhaustive searching and double-checking, which is not necessarily the norm, may represent an additional service, and a higher charge may be made as a result. If this is the service that you want, specify it and verify it:

Information provided will be accurate and material held will be as up to date as is available. Where it is essential that an exhaustive search for information takes place, the customer should inform the supplier when the request is placed. However, the supplier does not warrant that the material is fully accurate unless a specific request has been made to that effect and a warranty given to organization XYZ. It follows that neither the LIS nor its suppliers will be liable for the accuracy of information unless such a warranty has been specifically given to the user.

The next condition is to safeguard everyone against computer viruses. This is a major customer responsibility and you should ensure that the supplier enforces the necessary controls:

The customer must be personally satisfied that any electronic media supplied are free from virus infection. While the supplier and the LIS will check all media before use, no guarantee is given, especially not in respect of any media supplied by a third party (e.g. with a book or periodical subscription).

Now, we suggest some statements that are more specifically connected with the handling of enquiries and the provision of an LIS collection:

A comprehensive collection of material relevant to customers' information needs will be maintained. Customer needs will be systematically surveyed at intervals of 00 months.

Copies of the LIS collection development policy will be provided on request in connection with this initiative.

You will need to ensure that appropriate mechanisms are in place to carry out this function.

The next statement relates to the competence of both professional and paraprofessional LIS staff, and represents a commitment to training. It may be appropriate, depending on the organization's policy, to include reference to S/NVQs; or *The Investors in People Standard* (Investors in People UK, 1996), widely adopted in business, government and other organizations which place emphasis on the value of training; or a professional scheme such as The Library Association's professional development profile (Library Association, 1992); or the profiles contained in the British Computer Society's *Industry Structure Model*. For example:

> The supplier's staff will be trained appropriately to use the LIS resources of organization.XYZ. The customer's staff will be guided in the use of LIS resources (tours, demonstrations) at the beginning of this agreement and thereafter on request.

Turnaround times

Now we set out suggested turnaround times. The service specification contained in tender documents may impose a more complicated structure than this, involving different standards for different customers (e.g. a one-hour response for senior management). If the time to respond is set out in an invitation-to-tender document, it may be possible to refer to this, but it may be most satisfactory to repeat the service levels within the agreement document. Unless the times are varied at each review, it is reasonable to place this information in the body of the agreement rather than in an annexe:

> Enquiries from the organization's staff will be responded to within one working day. Enquiries expected to take longer than this will be carried out within an agreed timetable. Enquirers will be kept informed of progress.

A final paragraph in this section should deal with services to the public. It may be appropriate to include copies of the form used to handle public enquiries in an annexe. For example

> Enquiries from members of the public that fall within the agreed parameters for LIS services (stated in Annexe G to this agreement, as

and if amended by Annexe H) will be answered as quickly as possible. A response will be given to all telephone enquiries within one working day. The LIS will try to answer these enquiries from its own resources and, if it cannot help, try to suggest an alternative source of information. Ninety per cent of written enquiries will be answered within ten working days. Letters that cannot be answered within these limits will be acknowledged. Enquiries falling outside the current parameters for service will receive a courteous note within five working days referring them to public libraries or other appropriate sources.

If your organization is subject to the provisions of the Freedom of Information Act 2000, ensure that the required response standards are set out in the agreement.

Loans

The next function to be included is loans. There may be more complex standards than in our example if particular user groups are entitled to a higher (or lower) level of service. A basic approach is:

All requests will be responded to either by: (a) the despatch of the available publication within two working days; or (b) an acknowledgement of the request, together with a statement of the action taken and an estimate of the expected delivery date.

When delivery is not possible within six months (e.g. because of the delayed publication of a new title, or heavy demand for a scarce publication), the LIS will consult with the user to determine what further action should be taken.

[Loans will be despatched by first class post / internal post unless otherwise agreed with the customer.]

[Postage [above the second class rate] will be charged at the appropriate rate in the monthly customer account.]

[The use of a courier service is available at cost for very urgent requests.]

[The customer may collect very urgently required documents from the supplier's premises at High Street, Anytown.]

Clearly, some kind of monitoring process will be required to ensure that the deadlines are met. It is also wise to indicate to the customer those areas over which the LIS has control and those that are in the hands of the book trade or publishers. However, a commitment such as the following will make the role of the LIS clearer:

Publications that have waiting lists and those that are overdue will be chased regularly [at intervals of 00 weeks].

In a similar way, a statement is required to describe the handling of interlibrary loans. The second paragraph may be inappropriate in an LIS that operates primarily by obtaining materials on demand rather than by maintaining its own large stock of documents. For example:

Interlibrary loan requests will be processed within two working days of receipt. Specified deadlines will be met and all requests not supplied within ten working days will be reviewed. Customers will be kept informed of the progress of requests. The supplier will use its best endeavours but cannot influence the lending or copying policies, or the speed of service, of other libraries.

A target of 85% of loans will be satisfied from the internal stock of the LIS.

Other services

The following sections contain typical statements relating to the standards for other services.

105

Online searching

If requested, online searches will be carried out within one working day of receiving the request, otherwise searches are carried out and the results supplied within three working days. If the search is needed urgently, every effort will be made to meet the deadline. If more time is necessary, then a timetable will be agreed with the enquirer.

Printouts from the following databases will be provided on the same day unless agreed otherwise: [list services here].

Printouts from the following databases will be provided within one week unless agreed otherwise, especially if needed more urgently: [list services here; this group is intended for use when offline printing is significantly cheaper than the cost of printing the same information online].

Photocopies

Photocopies from the LIS stock will be supplied within five working days when the item is not on circulation or loan. Any deadline shorter than this will be met. Copyright restrictions on the supply of this material will be observed.

The LIS will endeavour to obtain 85% of photocopies from external sources within seven working days. Every effort will be made to meet deadlines. Customers will be kept informed of the progress of their request.

Materials for retention

Ninety per cent of retention requests will be passed to the acquisitions section for ordering within one working day, the rest within three working days, or they will be passed back to the requester within the same timescale.

Where delivery is not possible within six months (e.g. because of delayed publication of a new title, or heavy demand for a scarce publication), the supplier will consult the issuer of the request to determine what further action should be taken.

The terms above reflect closely those of other paragraphs, but it is important to show the terms that apply to each service, even at the expense of repetition. This will avoid the possibility of the supplier, or the customer, believing that different conditions and levels of service are acceptable.

Journals on circulation

Periodicals supplied on subscription will normally be supplied for a minimum of one calendar year. Before renewal instructions are issued, the supplier will issue a notice to registered users of the periodical to judge the likely future demand. Refunds of subscriptions are not normally available after annual renewal. The [LIS] [supplier] reserves the right to cancel a subscription if there is insufficient demand or if insufficient users respond to an enquiry.

All periodical parts received by the supplier will be checked-in and [circulated]/[posted for circulation] within one working day of receipt for items published at monthly intervals or more frequently, or two working days for other materials. Queries will be passed to [job name or role] and will be resolved within two weeks or as soon as the supplier replies.

Reading lists and bibliographical checking

Advice and a bibliographical service will be provided for departments in the organization requiring assistance with book lists.

Reading lists will be produced for departments from LIS and external resources as requested and within an agreed timetable.

Database quality management

Controls and procedures will be established, applied and monitored to ensure that all records on the internally created databases made available to customers meet minimum standards of quality, including accuracy and completeness.

Consider linking this point to requirements for standards of indexing and abstracting, or at least make sure that there is consistency between the two.

Housekeeping standards of service

The supplier will maintain a pleasant and safe working environment. The LIS will be tidied daily and the supplier's staff will ensure that cleaning takes place as scheduled. Areas will be maintained for reading and working with documents. The maintenance department will be contacted about shortcomings, faults and any other matters as necessary.

LIS materials will be reshelved daily and readers' tables cleared daily. Display racks and noticeboards will be checked regularly to remove out-of-date material.

Journals will normally be scanned for the database within three working days, except weekly journals which will normally be scanned within one working day.

Accurate statistics will be provided within the timetable agreed.

Stock will be kept in good order and in a satisfactory condition. Loose-leaf publications will be regularly updated.

Reading lists will be updated as new publications arrive. These lists will be displayed in the LIS where space allows.

Summary

We hope that the ideas above have helped you to see how important it is to spell out and keep updating the details in your agreement. It's likely that your own agreement will need to include other factors depending on your work sector. Remember that only by adhering to the agreement levels with your customers and monitoring the service provided by your supplier(s) will you be able to keep your services cost-effective and efficient. The initial agreement should therefore reflect attainable, if flexible, targets on all sides, or liaison between the organization, the LIS and the supplier will deteriorate into regular sessions of explanations and excuses. This is hardly a useful relationship for any of the parties.

9

Keeping the agreement on target

This chapter looks at:

- service monitoring
- the people who should be involved
- contents of monitoring reports
- review meetings between the parties
- service failure
- acting on the reports
- settling in
- dealing with recurring problems.

Service monitoring

Obviously you and your supplier (or suppliers) will want to keep the agreement between you on target and working to the advantage of all parties. To do this you will need to implement a service-monitoring regime that will provide the information which assures both you and the supplier that your arrangements are operating satisfactorily.

We suggested some measures of service delivery in our book on service level agreements (Pantry and Griffiths, 2001), and many of them can be applied to an outsourcing contract. Standard of delivery will be a key factor, and we recommend a graphic format for the report – or at least the summary – that will make it easy to assimilate the contents rapidly.

While a single set of measurements is unlikely to be of great use in determining how the outsourcing arrangement is performing, the regular reporting of information gives all parties an opportunity to examine the evidence and propose any changes needed.

An agreed regime of monitoring, reporting and adjustment is the best way of ensuring that the terms of the contract, and its performance, meet your requirements and the supplier's need to make a reasonable return on investment.

The people who should be involved

Arrangements with outsourcers may be subject to commercial confidentiality, so it may not be easy to make every item of information public, as would be done with an internal service level agreement.

This is an issue you will need to consider carefully in the context of freedom of information. One way of dealing with it is to declare sensitive information in ranges rather than as absolute values. For example, you could say that bids for journals provision were received ranging between £39,000 and £48,750 a year, rather than saying that you accepted a bid of £40,660. This will give some clues to the bidders: the cheapest bidder will guess that there were other issues such as delivery standards, and the bidder at £48,750 would either have to reduce overheads by a large margin, or be less greedy next time. But such a statement will protect the commercial interests of your selected supplier.

We mention the similarities and differences between outsourcing and service level agreements in various places throughout this book. An important point is to ensure that, if you have both types of agreement, you pay due regard to keeping the two in step with one another, so that you do not promise your internal clients a standard of service that your supplier is not contracted to provide. Going a step further, consider the relationship between the management of the two and whether a single person should fill the manager role for both agreements, or whether there should be common personnel between the two management teams.

From the supplier side it is useful to have a constant point of contact who can get to know the client organization well: this can smooth the way in case of difficulties, and can also build the kind of confidence that allows the supplier to suggest solutions based on a knowledge of the client's operations and culture.

Contents of monitoring reports

Presentation of service achievements in the form of a list of numbers is not helpful, especially as without an indication of performance against target it is not easy to see where problems lie by looking down a column of numerical indicators. To return to an example quoted in Chapter 7, the Fargo Public Library board decided to remove its outsourcing contractor not because of consistent underperformance, which might have shown up in a numerical display, but because it underperformed to a business- and reputation-threatening level on a single issue, the renewal of journal and newspaper subscriptions.

Reports of the numbers of items processed will be needed to verify the supplier's charges for those activities that are charged on a unit basis rather than as subscription items, so may have rather more relevance than in a standard SLA situation. But trends are equally important and it may be possible to spot a developing issue with the supplier's service before it becomes a major problem. The reports may also suggest whether there is an area of work that may sit badly with the outsourcing agreement and which may need to be managed in a different way (and which could thus be renegotiated by agreement or at the next renewal date).

Review meetings between the parties

It is a good idea to maintain the communication lines between yourself and your supplier by means of regular meetings. These ensure that any problems are brought to the attention of the other party or parties at an early date, and provide a ready-made structure where difficulties can be raised in a less confrontational arena than in a meeting called to deal specifically with a problem.

The supplier representative can attend these meetings to present information about latest performance, new services, and so forth. But offering this place as of right rather than on an ad hoc basis may alter the relationship with the supplier so that it becomes more difficult to manage in case of default. It may be as effective generally for the internal library committee to meet at regular and comparatively frequent intervals and to invite the supplier to every second or third meeting, or to attend part of a meeting only.

Service failure

The definition of service failure needs to be carefully crafted, especially if you have also set out various levels of severity in internal documents. A similar classification of the levels of severity will make it easier to decide how to deal with service failure. What impact will supplier service failure have on the operation of your service? Will it prevent any use of the service, in which case it could be categorized as high severity? Or will use of the service be possible but with reduced levels of efficiency, making that event a medium- or low-severity incident?

With the levels of severity defined, what steps must the contractor make to resolve the problem? And what is the maximum time allowable for the action to be taken? What steps will the supplier take to ensure there is no repetition, and how soon will these be in place?

Since service failure is such a critical incident in the relationship between the supplier and the customer it is important that all these steps are well defined.

The following suggested definitions are based on our recommendations for service level management (Pantry and Griffiths, 2001), making it possible to align the two sets of wording for the most effective co-ordination between your internal services and your outsourced supplies.

The service specifications will change depending on the level of outsourcing taking place: a failure in journals supply is unlikely to cause total loss of use of the LIS, but for a fully outsourced service a definition of critical failure is essential.

Service failure may be defined as:

1   Service failure is the inability to provide the services required or the inability to provide them to the specified standards, as set out in points 3 to 5.

2   Service failures will be rectified as soon as possible and in any case within the timescale set out in points 3 to 5 below.

3   Critical service delivery failure means the complete loss of service in one or more locations or any problem otherwise preventing customers from effective use of the LIS for longer than 15 minutes. The supplier will report to the customer within five minutes in response to reports of critical service delivery failure, detailing recovery procedures and stating the expected time of recovery.

4   Major service delivery failure means the partial loss of service in one location or any problem that will prevent customers from the effective use of any part of the LIS for longer than one hour. The supplier will report to the customer within 30 minutes in response to reports of major service delivery failure, detailing recovery procedures and stating the expected time of recovery.

5   Minor service delivery failure means any other failure of the system or closure of any part of the LIS that prevents efficient use. The supplier will report to the customer within four hours in response to

reports of minor service delivery failure, detailing recovery procedures and stating the expected time of recovery.

6 If the monitoring of service levels identifies a continuing failure on the part of the supplier to provide the required level of service, then the supplier will prepare, within one month of notice, a statement outlining the plan, for agreement with the customer, by which the service will be improved in order to meet the service targets in future. The supplier will report to the customer on progress at weekly intervals during the implementation of such a plan.

7 If service failures highlight consistent failure by a third-party supplier to meet service requirements, the outsourced supplier will prepare a report to the contract manager in the LIS recommending any changes of supplier, the use of penalty clauses, or other action to be taken to restore service.

8 Service performance failure shall be considered to have taken place if any major performance indicator [listed in an annexe] varies from target by more than the tolerances listed in points 9 to 11 below.

9 Service performance failure shall be considered to have taken place if in any financial year more than one of the performance indicators listed is more than 5% below target without prior agreement.

10 Service performance failure shall be considered to have taken place if in any financial year the supplier fails without prior agreement to achieve in excess of 80% of targets at all quarterly reports.

11 Service performance failure shall be considered to have taken place if in any financial year the number of complaints received from users exceeds 0.01% of the total number of transactions taking place in the LIS.

12 Penalties for service failure that is not remedied within the stated period, or which exceeds the stated tolerances, are set out at [reference].

Acting on the reports

If the supplier produces reports on a regular basis, it is essential for you to act upon them as soon as possible. Otherwise it could be argued that you were tolerating service failure and should not be able subsequently to claim damages or terminate the contract.

When reaching agreement with the supplier make it clear how you will review the reports. For example, does the contract manager have sole discretion, or would he or she need to consult a committee before recommending that penalties should be imposed? What is the timescale for this – does the committee need to meet, or can it take decisions by e-mail consultation? (You would probably want a proper meeting if you were recommending termination of the contract, but are these busy people who would find it difficult to make an emergency meeting?)

We have recommended meetings with suppliers as a more constructive and less confrontational way of managing the relationship, although you will need to remember that in a difficult negotiation it is your customers' requirements that all parties should be trying to meet. Both the contract manager's and the supplier's wish for a quiet life and maximum profit are secondary to that need – although, as we shall see in a moment, it should not be a problem to satisfy all of these needs almost all of the time.

The LIS contract manager must let the supplier know that the reports are being properly examined and not simply filed away on receipt. Raise issues that are highlighted by the supplier and ensure that the LIS management team understands them. This may simplify matters with the LIS committee when it is examining contract issues, or avoid the need to escalate matters to them. Changing suppliers is a time-consuming and difficult matter to manage, so that resolving difficulties through negotiation and discussion is preferable to a sudden decision to sack the existing service provider because of something that should have been picked up far earlier.

Settling in

The early days of the relationship between supplier and client are among the most difficult, as they either get used to working with each other for the first time or get used to a relationship that is more formalized than the traditional one between library and supplier. During this settling-in period you may decide that tolerances can be increased.

However, you need to balance this temporarily increased tolerance with the 'first impression' that you want the service to give. Think of your own experience when there has been a change of caterer at a refreshment facility that you use – in your organization if it is big, at your local coffee bar if yours is a small workplace. Were the first few days chaotic, with the staff telling you that things would improve when they were used to the equipment, or were you impressed with the quality and professionalism of the new team? If the new team was the old team in different uniforms, did its members seem proud to be part of the new organization, or did they hark back frequently to the old company? What did your experience tell you about the way your LIS should operate?

So allow for potential problems during the settling-in period. Be open about the difficulties and use your communications strategy (see Chapter 12) to let your customers know what is happening – how some things have changed and how other things are still the same. Decide whether you are more concerned to have a high level of service from the first day – which may be essential in some areas of business such as finance or hard science – or whether you will allow the contractor a short period of grace before considering penalties for underperformance.

Above all, agree and record what you decide so that there can be no come-back at a later date, either by the supplier or by your management committee.

Dealing with recurring problems

With all of these safeguards and procedures in place, you should be in a position to deal with any recurrent problems (such as consistent failure to place subscriptions, or unacceptable response times from outsourced systems) before they become major bones of contention between you and the supplier. However, you cannot ignore recurrent problems: otherwise they will become too big to resolve without threatening your entire relationship with the supplier. So why are there recurrent issues?

- **Is the specification wrong?** Has the supplier agreed to take on or been set a task that is impossible to achieve at the cost and quality stated? If so, change control is needed to agree a new way forward and get all parties signed up to the revised formula.
- **Is there a problem with a third party?** Perhaps the telephone company may not be providing the necessary bandwidth, or the delivery service fails to get materials to the LIS: (Note that this may not indicate bad service by the supplier but the wrong service may have been specified, such as 512Kb broadband when a 2Mb connection is needed for the volume of traffic carried.) Once again, renegotiation is needed, although in many instances it will be for the supplier to undertake this negotiation and probably to absorb any costs if its bid was poorly formulated and accepted by you in good faith. (This is an indication that you need to keep your legal advisers informed.)
- **Is there a problem about your expectations?** Has the LIS operation been re-engineered in a way that your staff or your customers do not fully understand? In this case, the answer is improved communication, and perhaps some additional training. Customers and staff need to understand what they are (and are not) entitled to under the contract, and that they may be causing problems by continuing to demand services or standards that it has been agreed are no longer wanted – or no longer affordable.
- **Is there a problem with the supplier?** When the other possibilities have been examined and dismissed, then you should be reminding the supplier of his responsibilities or contractual obligations, and setting

a timetable for remedy. But do be sure that you have looked at the other possibilities before you berate the supplier.

Summary

In this chapter we have looked at a wide variety of issues concerned with keeping the agreement running smoothly. We have emphasized our belief in a combination of amicable working with the supplier and ensuring that contractual obligations are met. We also reminded you that the service specification needs to make clear what is expected, and therefore has to give definitions of service failure and remedies. But the main message is that none of these issues is a show stopper and, if you specify clearly and work through the issues logically, you should be assured of both reliable service and a good relationship with a dependable outsourced supplier.

10

Keeping your users happy with the outsourced service

In this chapter we examine the importance of relationships with your users:

- what your customers want
- negotiating and agreeing the terms
- continual customer education
- providing feedback
- managing problems
- using the LIS properly
- telling your customers about people's responsibilities
- things to prevent
- service breakdown
- keeping in touch
- escalation
- change control
- supplier default issues.

Introduction

Why do we say that the LIS manager should manage users or customers of the service in order to keep them happy? By customer education (to create the so-called 'intelligent customer') you will avoid many problems in service provision. The user–customer, as one of the parties to the agreement, has expectations and assumptions about the service, which the LIS manager handles or even manipulates by a variety of means including outsourcing. If there are not to be any unpleasant surprises in operating through an outsourcing arrangement then the LIS manager must ensure that the customer is satisfied with it. This means the customer understanding what the service does not provide as well as what it does provide.

Benefits lie both in ensuring the smooth operation of the current agreement and in preparing for future changes to (or replacement of) the agreement. By the time of its eventual renewal, the customer's understanding of the LIS business should have improved to the point where real choices can be made and a more satisfactory agreement reached than for each previous period.

What the customer wants

Strictly speaking, it is not the supplier's task to define what the customer wants. The LIS manager is asked to agree a specification, and may well negotiate the terms available, but the definition must ultimately be the customer's, and not the supplier's. (This criticism was levelled particularly at the purchaser–provider relationship in the NHS.)

Suppliers are, however, at liberty to suggest what services they would like to provide. Some do so, for example by issuing model specifications which just happen to match the services they sell. Related to this is the problem that the range of outsourced services available is still fairly restricted, so that if, for example, you decide to go for an outsourced library management system, then users will have to accept the features of that system rather than demand features that belong to their ideal system. (It is therefore important that you decide carefully what are essential and what are desirable features of the systems or services that you outsource, and that your users or customers understand clearly why you have included as essential only those features that you know the market can currently provide.) If services, under the service management agreements that you have with your users, can be modified in line with changing need, then the agreement should also spell out the customers' rights and responsibilities, and address the issues of continuing service during negotiation and of the funding for the new services within the financial framework of the agreement.

Customers must feel that they have been fully consulted and that in effect they share the ownership of the service definition that is enshrined in the agreement. A focus group approach may work well here, bringing together representatives from different parts of the organization – possibly with differing or even conflicting requirements. They need to consider questions such as these – and agree answers:

- What features are needed in a library and information service for the organization (or in various services for different parts of it)?
- What value does each group attach to it, and what is their perception of its value to the organization as a whole?
- How much monetary value does the group attach to the service, and would it be willing to pay this amount if hard charging were introduced? (This is especially relevant to outsourcing, since real money will be changing hands and you may well decide to – or be forced to – hard charge for the services that are provided from outside your organization.)
- Which services will be a standard part of the LIS offer, and which ones optional (and charged) extras?
- What incentives would the users like to offer the LIS in order to develop services they require?

The LIS manager would be well armed in these negotiations with a copy of a service statement for the LIS that he or she operates. This specification is capable of expansion into the basis of an agreement with the users of the service, and provides them with a clear statement of what is already in the standard service offer that the LIS is prepared to procure from the outsourcer on behalf of the entire customer base. This avoids the need for the customer to invest time and effort in learning the definition of LIS terminology and makes it easier for the client side to develop an 'intelligent customer' function. But, as we have emphasized in other chapters, care has to be taken to define terminology very carefully. In this situation, the usual confusion between different senses of technical terms needs to be avoided, as does the use of LIS jargon, if disputes are to be avoided.

Using a service statement or brochures produced by the LIS, the customer's needs can be matched to specific services listed, or it can be explained how a service or combination of services will meet a particular customer need. It is often more useful to discover, as with the reference interview technique, what need the customer is trying to satisfy when describing a required service that the LIS does not have and does not wish to develop. Often, customers describe a process that they believe will deliver the required result, rather than a service they actually need. If the LIS works with the customer to define the need, it will serve two purposes: one is to define the requirement that is not currently met, which will provide the specification to be sent to potential providers to invite bids; the other is to feed into an internal service level agreement that will inform the way that customers use the outsourced services.

Negotiating and agreeing the terms

At the end of this process you should have arrived at some agreed statement of what the customer wants, couched in terms that can be passed to potential external suppliers, and that will satisfy the corporate legal department.

Many LIS staff seem to resent the time spent on the negotiation of the terms of agreements, saying they could use the time better by carrying out professional tasks. But the work on negotiation, as with time invested in user education, will save time later through the avoidance of disputes, and if elements of the service are to be supplied by a third party then it is absolutely essential that the time is taken. It can be a painstaking and tedious time, especially for early adopters. Not only are these customers who cannot be presented with agreements that have already been widely adopted, and which they will therefore be hard put to alter or substantially rewrite, they are also likely to be high-profile corporate users (or they certainly should be). This will give you additional leverage with the outsourcer since no supplier wants to inconvenience senior managers of any customer organization as a result of their poor service or inappropriate solutions to your information requirements. From the LIS manager's point of view there is a further benefit in signing up senior management and other large departments as early users of the outsourced service: starting with smaller customer groups is likely to throw up a lot of anomalies but will not address the core requirements of the company altogether.

Continual customer education
Feedback and information
Customers need to understand that using the LIS properly has benefits for both them and supplier. It follows that the LIS manager must give continual feedback and information to the customer on developments in LIS services. If an external 'expert' is used to prepare it, the service specification is particularly likely to define an LIS that is the affordable balance between cost and feasibility at the date of its preparation. Development in LIS continues at high speed. The world wide web, for example, went from being an interesting sideline to an essential information tool in less than the average life of a LIS contract. The LIS manager must provide users with sufficient knowledge to review the specification whenever necessary, and must encourage this process. It is to no one's advantage for customers to find that a more up-to-date service would have suited them better. The LIS manager will fall behind the field, while the customer's

reaction to such a discovery may well be to blame the LIS manager for failing to point out the shortfalls.

New initiatives and products

An hour spent in user education may save several more being wasted later on in resolving complaints. Frequent presentations may be one way of achieving this, perhaps as part of the liaison meetings where a standard agenda item might be 'service developments and new products'. This would allow the presentation of new initiatives from the LIS and give time for suppliers to present their products (free of charge, of course), thus enhancing further the reputation of the LIS for being at the leading edge of development. Your existing outsourcers will probably be pleased to take up such an opportunity, although it would be good business practice as well as simply fairer to also invite potential suppliers to demonstrate what is possible using their products.

Intellectual property rights

Customers also need to understand and appreciate the full implications of working within the copyright and other intellectual property laws, and once again time spent in education will be amply repaid through the avoidance of disputes. This becomes more important still where application service providers (ASPs) are employed, since customers may infringe the intellectual property rights of others with whom the contractual arrangement is managed by the LIS. The SLA needs to highlight that in these instances the responsibility is the customer's, and perhaps to state explicitly the terms of indemnification. While this may be somewhat academic where ultimately the legal responsibility falls on a named individual such as the company secretary who is not a member of the LIS or of the offending section, how far the liability of the LIS extends must be clearly stated.

Training

Customers should be encouraged to ask for training where necessary: for example, how to use computerized services or contact the outsourcer. They also need to understand that they must manage the use of passwords to get into the services in a responsible manner. The LIS must ensure that the customer understands the reasons for this, especially important if hard charging for the outsourced service is in force. The LIS must ensure that the customer understands the control mechanisms that govern the LIS budget.

Providing feedback

A recognized two-way channel for feedback between the supplier and the customer is essential. If there are difficulties, the supplier should not have to guess why an agreement is under threat or a breach alleged, so there needs at least to be a means of channelling complaints and ensuring their resolution. It is worth having a clause insisting that this procedure is exhausted before a breach is signalled. This usually entails both the customer and the supplier mirroring each other's organization by providing named points of contact at various levels in their hierarchies, and specifying escalation procedures.

We have often heard it said that LIS suppliers prefer to deal with librarians than with procurement staff who are handling a library contract because librarians and LIS suppliers both speak the same language and both understand the business of libraries. This is very pertinent in this context: while it may not be possible, or indeed appropriate, for the LIS and the supplier to establish a line of communication that excludes the contract manager, there needs to be an arrangement that allows the LIS and supplier management teams to interact – probably in a forum involving the procurement specialists – to exchange views on the operation of the LIS functions covered by the outsourcing agreement.

Engaging the customer in a continuous dialogue can be very helpful in shaping and delivering the type of service. Ensuring that the customers' needs are fully understood can be usefully achieved through encouraging feedback, whether good or bad. The process can reinforce messages about their own responsibilities, for example, in alerting the LIS of any changes in their requirements. This could be a new area of work for the customers, changes of direction, new staff needing different levels of information. The 'how', 'why', 'when', 'to whom', and so on should be written into the internal SLA and reflected in the outsourcing agreement.

There are further ways in which customer feedback can help the supplier deliver a better service. For example, subject specialists will be able to give warning of important new publications. Customers can also be 'managed' through a dialogue that encourages them to give the fullest details available for requests and enquiries. As the outsourcer is likely to rely on the LIS at least to confirm information, it is in both their interests for the LIS to manage internal customers to make the information flows as reliable as possible.

Customer surveys are a sound means of ensuring that feedback is obtained. A quarterly review will give an opportunity to ask specific questions about under- or over-used services, as well as a basket of broader regular enquiries about user satisfaction and requirements. Adding sufficient space for comments, or enquiring about developing requirements in an open question, will provide early warning of fresh needs or emerging difficulties.

Feedback from the customer should also include warnings of unusual workloads, such as those arising from new projects. Normal volumes of work should be defined in the service specification, together with an agreed ceiling for peak loads above which deadlines and costs become negotiable outside the agreement proper. This allows the LIS manager to schedule resources more effectively and to remain within budget while being flexible in meeting the customer's new requirements, and to involve the outsourcer in costing and implementing arrangements for meeting these demands.

In the other direction, formalized feedback helps the LIS manager by providing a channel for news of success in meeting targets, highlighting potentially useful developments in LIS work, and so forth.

Feedback has one other benefit: it helps to eliminate nasty surprises, which otherwise occur at contract review meetings. Suppliers must be able to plan and deliver the services to schedule and operate profitably or at least within budget, and they do not like nasty surprises any more than the members of your own organization.

Managing problems

Sooner or later some kind of problem will occur involving the customers of one of your outsourced services. We saw above that this may arise because of:

- **Demand**: something new, which the customer wants done and the LIS has not elected or contracted to provide
- **Expectation**: something the customer thought would be done but which the LIS does not consider has been specified, and has not therefore put in place a contract to supply
- **Perception**: something that the customer expected to be done but which the supplier did in a different way, or at a different time or to a different level.

All problems become worse if they are left to fester. The LIS manager must insist that any perceived shortfalls are reported to the LIS help desk as soon as possible. The help desk has three functions at this point, contributing to the aims of both calming and resolving. The first is to establish that there really is a fault or shortfall, so that the LIS can set remedial action in train. The second is to dissuade the customer from carrying out a do-it-yourself fix on the problem, and possibly making it worse. The third, and potentially most important, is to stop the customers from ringing the outsourced supplier direct and giving them hell. (Unless of course you have contracted the help-desk function to the supplier, in which case it may wish things were otherwise!)

Your help-desk staff need to display tact. At first they will be working to educate users, since the answer to many queries will be contained in documentation held by the customer. They also need to be flexible. No useful purpose is served when they use their SLA as a fixed statement of services they are permitted to offer, and refuse to consider how other demands can be met, even if the customer offers payment that could be used to negotiate further services from the outsourcer. The customer is not pleased to be told what could have been done, if only the service had not been outsourced.

Using the LIS properly

Customers cannot truly complain if the service they have specified turns out to be inadequate when procured and supplied by the LIS. If this happens it may be useful to reinforce messages on the proper use of the LIS and its facilities, to ensure that no customers decide to alter the rules in their favour in an attempt to improve matters, such as concluding their own deals with external suppliers. Without such insistence, it may be difficult to operate the LIS within financial or other targets and it may also breach the commercial agreements made with the outsourcer. The answer to such a situation must be to negotiate changes to suit all parties. An 'I told you so' response from LIS staff is unlikely to win new friends but it is reasonable to insist that the LIS customers stick to the existing agreements until the changes are implemented.

This certainly must extend to the use of passwords, LIS pass cards, and similar means of controlling access and costs. 'No card, no service' is a suitably memorable slogan. Another important lesson is that, if you give your access code to someone else, you pay when they use it. The LIS cannot operate in a hard charging regime if it constantly has to transfer charges between accounts or has to argue about who actually used the service,

while the outsourcer must be able to assume that anyone using its services has authority to do so, in terms of both management and budget. The
LIS must insist on being treated no differently from other parts of the
organization in this respect, and should point out what ructions there would
be if, for example, it came to a separate agreement with a cleaning company because the existing facilities management didn't suit the LIS
managers, and what further mayhem would follow if it then refused to
pay for the new firm of cleaners.

If there are local rules relating to levels of authority needed to order
publications, copying, printing, etc., these should also appear both in internal SLAs and in contract documentation with the outsourcing supplier
for the avoidance of doubt on anyone's part. Nor should the LIS lose any
opportunities to insist that statutory responsibilities under a range of legislation (including intellectual property and freedom of information) lie
with the end-user. It would be useful to have a common approach agreed
with other internal suppliers such as the archives service and with external suppliers. You will probably want to check this policy with your lawyers;
your outsourcing suppliers should involve their legal departments as well.

Telling your customers about people's responsibilities

It is essential to make users aware of which services that the LIS might
be expected to perform directly are in fact outsourced. If these are the
direct responsibility of the outsourcer and are offered as additional services, your customers need to know the contact names and numbers, and
what arrangements they are responsible for making to ensure payment.
Keep a list of such issues (perhaps as a page on your intranet) and make
sure it is revised regularly with the latest policies. Here are some possible examples of this type of service:

- updating loose-leaf publications
- checking receipt of periodicals that are delivered directly to users

- distributing press copies of the organization's publications
- delivering afternoon newspapers, especially multiple editions.

If your outsourcer produces publications for you based on information managed by you, customers who input to those publications have responsibilities that also need to be highlighted. Is there a code or manual that has to be applied in data entry? Must a particular thesaurus or cataloguing code be applied? Whose responsibility is it to edit inadequate entries to meet the standard and who accepts the cost if an entry is rejected by an external buyer of the resulting records?

You will also need to specify some everyday responsibilities, such as telling the LIS when people move offices, so that this does not lead to a dispute with the supplier over wasted part-subscriptions or over apparent delays in delivery to a new address. More LIS-orientated responsibilities must include rules such as taking responsibility for materials handed to other users without passing back through the LIS and, in particular, taking financial responsibility for lost or overdue materials that are the property of the outsourced supplier. In particular, customers must acknowledge that their behaviour may affect the entire organization and its contractual relationship with the external supplier. This extends an insistence that only the LIS may place orders with suppliers, and that departments placing irregular orders must pay the invoice. Perhaps it should also be made clear that the LIS role does not extend to haranguing the external supplier if it declines to accept ad hoc telephone orders from senior members of staff determined to get round the rules!

Legal constraints

Both LIS and suppliers are used to working under various legal constraints, but general users are, arguably, not aware of them. Agreements therefore need to echo (by reference to other documents rather than by exhaustive listing) the requirements affecting the LIS. In particular, there should be references to copyright regulations (bearing in mind that librarians may have privileges not granted to the rest of the organization). It may be worth referring to all the licensing organizations with whom the parent body has concluded agreements. Other licence agreements should also be referred to, such as those commonly attached to computer discs and CD-ROMs bound into books. This may also be a useful place to insert conditions relating to safeguarding against computer viruses. Sharing this information with suppliers will ensure that potential costly errors are avoided.

Things to prevent

In an operational regime that employs outsourced LIS suppliers, safeguards are needed to provide the LIS with stability and protection, and customers should be required to sign up to them. This means that internal SLAs should contain an agreement not to attempt to purchase other LIS services, such as a new business reference service. It may be more difficult to get agreement that members of your organization will not be allowed to access electronic information resources directly, and indeed you may well not want to restrict this access.

Service breakdown

In an organization managed by contracts and agreements, the LIS may find it has few sanctions when members of the organization break agreements. Can you really cut off users who make additional contracts outside those managed by the LIS? Is the LIS in breach of its agreement if it does so?

You should consider the circumstances in which the agreements would be suspended. For example, if a breakdown in outgoing telecommunications means that the organization loses contact with the outsourcing supplier and service is not delivered, who accepts responsibility? If the organization suffers a power failure and cannot access the supplier's services, is the supplier's performance still to be monitored until contact is restored? We recommend that where central services, such as power, heating and lighting are supplied by the organization, the LIS SLA should specify failure of those services as a reason to suspend service measurement. So it would be sensible to look at factors such as these that could affect communication with the outsourcer, and agree which would cause the measurement of the outsourcing agreement to be suspended.

The agreement could include definitions of severity levels. Is a problem trivial or does it prevent any work until it is resolved? How soon does it need to be fixed? These levels should be used in completing the help-desk logs, which the LIS manager should review regularly with the contract manager.

Remember that the time to fix may be more important to one group of your customers than to another. It may be that you have to argue for different severity levels for the same problem at various times of the day or week in order to reflect priorities realistically – for example, it may be more important to ensure that news cuttings have arrived on a Monday morning because a board meeting takes place then and reviews the financial tips in the Sunday press.

Keeping in touch

Regular meetings between the parties – the LIS, the outsourcer, the procurement and finance team, and the customer user group – will ensure that many of these issues can be managed easily. Meetings should be frequent enough to allow problems to be resolved before they become difficult to handle. On the other hand, it is useful for them to be sufficiently well spaced to allow comprehensive new reports on service achievements to be presented to each meeting.

These meetings will help to identify key players (and their deputies) from each side and keep them in personal contact, helping to avoid confrontation. They should be focused on service development and the reporting of successful achievement, rather than on examining shortfalls and failures of service. The help-desk logs will provide useful information for these meetings.

The supplier may wish to use these meetings to present future plans. While many people at the meeting would resent a straight sales pitch, the supplier does need to know that planned investment will be worthwhile, or that products under development are worth bringing to market because customers will have a use for them. So a balance needs to be struck, and perhaps agreement reached that the supplier can make a presentation on planned new products on one or two occasions a year.

Escalation

The agreement with the outsourcer should set out escalation procedures for the resolution of disputes when the parties cannot agree. Normally, this will mean the managers on each side have a problem that they cannot amicably resolve between them. If resolution cannot be achieved, the issue goes a stage further up each managerial line. Usually the contract or agreement allows for a final arbiter to be consulted if senior managers cannot reach agreement.

This arrangement is mirrored where internal service level agreements are in place, but care must then be taken to ensure that the escalation procedures are set out to avoid conflicts of interest at the senior levels of your organization. You should not have any problem in this respect with outsourcing agreements except in the fairly unlikely event that your outsourced supplier is in fact another part of your organization. One of our case studies looks at an outsourcing supplier that is jointly owned by a number of libraries in Washington, DC, but as the supplier is a separate company from any of its customers, they should have no complications of this nature. But some of the general principles of SLA management should still apply to outsourcing.

The most senior manager to whom problems can be escalated should be named. Similarly, the name of the most senior manager on the supplier side should be published. If one of these people moves, change control should be invoked to name the replacement in the agreement, although you could and should reduce this need by specifying the post rather than naming the postholder as far as possible.

Change control

Agreements that cast in stone the services being delivered are of little lasting use. Therefore, a system of change control is required, to allow amendments, deletions and additions to be made to reflect current requirements and resources. Without it, unsatisfactory clauses cannot be changed and a satisfactory contract cannot be extended without a complete re-tendering exercise. The agreement should therefore say what procedures need to be followed and how they (and the agreement reached) are recorded. It should be stated whether changes have to be made by mutual consent, or whether one party can agree changes with a third party, such as a management board, and bypass the other party's contract managers.

Our recommendation on service level agreements is that the minor details that are likely to change at fairly frequent intervals (such as the names of responsible managers) should appear in an annexe to the agreement, while the main agreement contains key information that is likely to be valid throughout the period of the contract. The same applies to outsourcing agreements: consider what level of change is important enough to warrant calling together the entire change control committee to record agreement. If the information isn't as important as that then think about putting it into an annexe that can be updated by correspondence or e-mail.

Supplier default

You rely on many third parties, internally and externally, to deliver your service. These include your own suppliers, such as booksellers and journals agents, your internal messenger service, couriers and the postal authorities. Have you thought what would happen if one of them failed you – and whether this would have an effect on your other suppliers? For example, would your other suppliers be able to fill the void, and would you have to rely on their goodwill to avoid having to pay again for services or subscriptions you have already bought?

You need to be clear about whether the LIS would go on supplying a service to its customers in case of supplier default (and if so what level of service). Consider having a break clause inserted into your external contracts allowing you to take action if you suffer severe problems as a result of supplier default.

Case study

The subscription supplier divine, also known to many by its former names of Rowe.com and Faxon, notified customers of its intention to cease being a subscriptions agent and filed for Chapter 11 bankruptcy protection in late 2002 after it had taken payment for 2003 subscriptions from a number of its customers. As a result it did not pay publishers for all the subscriptions it had collected. This left a number of libraries in a difficult position. For example, the Library of Mount Holyoke College, the 'Seven Sisters' faculty in South Hadley, MA, posted the following message in its newsletter:

> Recently the library's long-time subscription agent, Faxon/Rowe Com notified the library of their intention to cease being a subscription agent and then filed Chapter 11 bankruptcy papers. As of today the company has taken the college's payment for subscription renewals but has failed to pay all the publishers for MHC 2003 subscriptions. The library staff is working hard to determine which titles are not renewed and may be forced to make some very difficult decisions in the coming months.
>
> www.mtholyoke.edu/lits/about/news/index.shtml

The Mount Holyoke librarian also wrote to the chairs of the College's departments asking them for ideas and comments on what could be done about the situation.

A large group of libraries and publishers has since formed a steering committee to investigate the financial conditions of Rowe.com and explore options to protect creditor interests. As at mid-2004, this private Yahoo! discussion group at groups.yahoo.com/group/rowecomcreditors/ has 1130 members who receive non-confidential information from the steering committee.

A number of professional groups also took on an active role in the crisis: for example, the Special Libraries Association operated a portal giving information such as updates on publishers who had decided to honour subscriptions placed through divine and librarians who were acting as liaison points for particular subscriptions; while the Medical Libraries Association provided a range of information for divine customers; and the discussion list liblicense-l@lists.yale.edu provided a discussion forum.

Although the Special Libraries Association has reorganized its website since this time and the divine and Rowe.com websites have been removed, you can track events by using the Wayback Machine at www.archive.org, and visiting the archived versions of www.divine.com, www.rowe.com, www.sla.org and www.mlanet.org.

Whatever the eventual conclusion that the library and financial communities reach over its underlying causes, the case study demonstrates that on occasion even a supplier of very long standing can experience catastrophic problems. These may not be directly to do with the company and its managers that you have long known, but can be a result of the mergers and acquisitions that have become increasingly commonplace in the world of library and information services supply. Indeed, if you use risk analysis (see below), one factor you should assess is the likelihood that your supplier is so successful that it may look like a cast-iron acquisition for another company that has other interests; this second company may decide to quit library supply in a business downturn.

The techniques of risk analysis could be useful here: assess what you know about your suppliers, and weight your assessment of the likelihood of their being unable to supply you in one, two or three years' time against the impact that this would have on your operations. See Table 10.1.

Table 10.1   Risk analysis for potential suppliers

Supplier	Product supplied	Risk	Impact	Score	Comments
'A'	Journals	2 (low)	10 (very high)	20	Family firm, long track record, has resisted previous takeovers.
'B'	Books	6 (medium)	8 (high)	48	Poor trading results last year, known to be target of chain buying up local bookshops. Other local libraries can recommend suitable alternative suppliers if B encounters major difficulties.
'C'	Telecoms	1 (very low)	10 (very high)	10	Campus network
'D'	Stationery	3 (low)	5 (medium)	15	Centrally managed framework. Some possible problems with specialist stationery but central procurement would be able to source alternatives.

The result should give you an indication of which supplies you should identify possible alternative suppliers for, not because you want to end the agreement with your existing supplier early, but in case the unexpected happens. In the fictitious example demonstrated in Table 10.1, you would want to look first at alternative book suppliers if you were worried that your supplier may be taken over by a larger company that wants to move bestselling paperbacks to the public rather than supply your college library, but could be more relaxed about other services and could expect your central administration to deal with failure of some of those suppliers.

Summary

Keeping customers informed and happy is an important element of outsourcing your services. Your service level agreements provide you with the opportunity to bind your customers to responsible behaviour by setting out in detail their commitments to the LIS and its suppliers. Although the section on customer responsibilities is usually one of the shortest parts of an agreement, it is among the most important, and so it needs to be carefully written. Use your management skills and business techniques to keep on top of the situation and be able to assure your customers that you are prepared for any eventuality.

After reading this chapter you should be considering how your internal and external agreements will reflect:

- what the customers' true requirements are, and the ways in which you will discover them
- what behaviour you expect of your customers, in the way they approach the LIS, in the way they choose to find information other than by using the LIS, and in the way they treat the outsourced supplier
- what steps you will take to maintain dialogue with suppliers, how you will convey the results to customers, and how you will manage the dialogue that captures your customers' requirements and convey these to the supplier

- what steps you will be taking to mitigate potential problems
- what education and training your users require in order to understand and meet their obligations.

11

Keeping staff happy with the outsourced service

In this chapter we examine the importance of relationships with your staff before and during the implementation of the outsourcing process:

- continual dialogue with staff
- managing staff attitudes
- avoiding conflict
- opportunities for all.

Continual dialogue with staff

The LIS manager should keep in close contact with all staff from the outset. It is vital that staff are involved in all aspects of discussions to avoid problems in service provision. The staff, as one of the parties to the agreement, have expectations, knowledge and assumptions about the service(s) which the LIS manager needs to outsource and manage. If there are not to be any unpleasant surprises in operating the agreement, the LIS manager must ensure that the staff understand what is being proposed for outsourcing as well as being satisfied with the proposals. This includes understanding what the service does not provide as well as what it does.

It will be useful for the staff to have a chance to 'sample' the outsourcing practices of other library and information services before making a commitment or a costly mistake. Outsourcing initially seems attractive to LIS decision makers, but at the same time they must be wary of its impact on in-house staff, productivity and quality. The manager must be able to answer a number of questions about outsourcing before signing a contract. Is outsourcing of the service(s) the most cost-effective alternative? What are the in-house implications of outsourcing? How will it affect the staff in-house? Will outsourcing actually free up staff to provide better services to users?

The management of staff is a vital element in your plans to introduce an outsourced service. If the staff are unwilling or unhappy, the introduction and operation of an outsourced service of any kind is likely to be beset by squabbles over petty interpretation of the details, and the service is likely to be affected by a sense of reduced co-operation and inflexibility. Customers will be sure to notice, and the positive benefits of the outsourced service will be overlooked as all parties struggle to overcome these negative aspects.

Consider your staff as being divided into two types: those who are active in spreading new ideas and ways of working, and those who are passive, and get their ideas by 'buying' them from other members of staff. The active staff – the opinion setters and the strong characters – can prove the most difficult if they take against working with outsourcers, so it pays to take care that they understand fully what the changes are all about. Frequently these are the people that form the links between the new contractor and the organization at large. If the contract is let in such a way that the LIS staff are the points of contact for outsourced services such as publications orders and other purchases, a difficult attitude or any expression of hostility towards the new arrangements will be immediately obvious to your customers, and quite probably to other members of your organization.

One reason for hostility may be that the new arrangements involve managing the transition from one type of service to another – this is just sheer hard work for the people at the front line. You need to acknowledge that in the transition period, and when the LIS customers are getting used to the new ways of working, there can be considerable stress involved which mere payment for the overtime hours will not necessarily address. Find some other way, involving money, time off, or extolling the staff efforts to the organization as a whole to show that you recognize their contribution.

The effects of outsourcing on LIS staff may be investigated by the following questions:

- What effect does organizational culture have on the outsourcing decision?
- If we outsource what will happen to the current staff?
- Can we outsource if we are unionized or our employees are employed by a public sector organization?
- Will outsourcing affect staff morale?
- How are staff likely to react to outsourcing?
- How much time will elapse between deciding to outsource and actual implementation?
- What assistance will be given to LIS staff to help them adjust?
- What steps will be taken to inform the staff?
- What will happen after the announcement about outsourcing is made?
- What if a staff member has to transfer to the outsource supplier – how will this be carried out?
- Are there alternatives for staff who don't want to transfer to the new supplier?

These questions can be anticipated and used in the various communication channels, e.g. in an 'outsourcing newsletter'.

Managing staff attitudes

Staff can cause various problems in the management of outsourced agreements.

Staff criticize the new system

Members of staff opposed to change may take every opportunity to tell customers that the new ways are not sensible, or get in the way of providing the kind of service that the library has traditionally given the customer. If these are key staff, this can quickly undermine the perception of the quality of the library, and begins to cast doubt on the soundness of management if an apparently unfavourable contract has been entered. Staff who are known to be critical in this fashion need to be handled tactfully but firmly. They must realize that the alternative is not to scrap the outsourced service but to find ways to manage it flexibly. It is essential, therefore, to keep staff aware of the progress of negotiations, so that they are prepared for the changes.

Staff adopt a 'no-go' attitude

Members of staff may draw attention to the shortcomings of the new system, particularly its apparent inflexibilities, again telling customers that it is now beyond the staff's ability to provide the kind of service that used to be available. Rather than overt hostility, this type of behaviour tends towards a kind of conspiracy, in which the LIS staff and customers are seen to collude against the inept management that has agreed to such an inflexible arrangement. The awkward staff can further conspire with the customer to do a favour ('Just this once, then') that makes the customer into a client of the member of staff rather than of the LIS as a whole. Again, it is best to demonstrate the flexibility of the service from the outset, and ensure that customers as well as staff know that the existence of the agreement does not condemn every transaction to being a long drawn-out process that delays simple orders for weeks.

Criticism of the outsourced supplier

Particularly difficult is the member of staff who openly criticizes the new supplier. Sometimes this comes out in the form of adverse criticism ('We never had these problems with the old supplier'); otherwise it is straightforward moaning about anything that goes wrong, like incorrect billing. Suppliers are unlikely to be pleased if this gets back to them, and even less pleased if it gets to other organizations that are considering doing business with them. If there are problems, your staff must be objective, and ensure that those problems are sorted out. The supplier must have the chance to put things right – we are, after all, considering a contract which will have appropriate clauses to require and to allow this to happen. Staff need to be made aware that their first action when there are problems must be to get onto the supplier to correct matters, not to start criticizing.

'Us and them'

Most staff are quite happy to work together with a supplier and present a unified face to the LIS customer, so that when there are supply problems the user is left with the feeling that the LIS and the outsourced supplier are working together to solve them. Outsourcing can have the effect of creating a division in the customer's perception in what had previously been a single spectrum working to provide his or her information needs. It is now 'them' who are causing a problem by their failure to work to the same methods as the previous supplier, or 'us' who are having to put up with poor service which disappoints our customers.

As well as demonstrating flexibility, you may need to challenge members of staff who spread this kind of view. They need to see that there is no difference between the new relationship and that with a previous supplier. Suppliers are in business to succeed and – let's face it – to make a profit, and any company that consistently ignores the requirements of its customers will pretty soon fail. It may be hard going for a few weeks but both supplier and library have the same long-term aim. By creating division, your staff members are not giving your supplier a proper chance to resolve the difficulties.

Resentment over the work involved

The introduction of an outsourced service inevitably leads to some additional initial work. Or rather it leads to different tasks being done when others may no longer be needed. Your staff may not be servicing the books any longer by adding plastic covers or labels, or you may decide to accept cataloguing in publication information and let the supplier apply class labels accordingly. You may use some of the time saved to carry out a quality check on the supplier, perhaps by sampling every tenth item and performing checks on various elements of the servicing. The rest of the time saved can be put into new activities that generate further custom for the LIS, and make its position more secure. However, it can happen that the new work of checking becomes more noticeable than the saving of work passed to the supplier, or the value of the new work that others are doing with the saved time. It must be made clear what changes have taken place across the spectrum, so that staff can be pleased about the work they are saved (and the quality of the supplier's work, it must be hoped) rather than annoyed that they appear to have even more work. If work is properly designed, LIS staff will still have ultimate control, through the quality-checking process, of what is being delivered to the customer.

Difficulties fall to the LIS staff

Staff may perceive themselves as taking the blame for any shortcomings in the service(s), when previously a call to the supplier would probably have sorted matters out amicably and quickly. The outsourcing agreement should not act as a barrier to the LIS customer, who does not have a direct role in the agreement and cannot take complaints to the supplier directly. The fact that there is now a formal document setting out rights and responsibilities can also lead to entrenched attitudes being taken, and the LIS staff will find themselves in the position of needing to interpret the outsourced agreement for both the supplier ('What we meant by that clause was . . .') and the LIS user ('When they say this, what the suppliers mean is . . .'). Tactics for dealing with this should include a plan for communication with library customers, to explain how problems are to be resolved, and possibly a fast-track procedure for the quick resolution of major problems. Simple tactics often succeed quickly, such as rostering staff to ensure that the same person does not always handle complaints.

'Eating into professional time'

We have encountered professional staff who consider that contract management interferes with the 'real' work of a qualified librarian, and should be left to support staff or accountants. There is not really a remedy for dealing with this attitude, other than to record that, in the 21st century, this is part of what LIS management is about. Managers need to demonstrate their ability to deliver best value for money, and to monitor the way that they do this: outsourcing agreements and service level agreements are good tools for doing so, and there is no excuse for attitudes like this.

TUPE

The results of the TUPE process – the transfer of staff from the LIS to supplier or other employer under the Transfer of Undertakings (Protection of Employment) Regulations – can also produce staff problems. This is a difficult problem for library managers, particularly if part of the LIS team is being moved compulsorily. Staff being transferred must be seen to be getting the best deal possible, and if you can offer them the choice of whether to transfer or be moved to different work that is remaining in-house, it may be an easier process to manage.

Avoiding conflict
Training

The best way of averting difficulties is to ensure that everyone on your staff is fully aware of what is happening. Training schemes will explain what changes are taking place, and why. This is entirely in the spirit of many of the systems currently used by large organizations to demonstrate their management quality, such as the Investors in People standard or the Charter Mark. It could be useful to provide specific training for your staff on management of both in-house and outsourced service levels, bringing together a cross-section of types and seniority of staff where possible. Improved internal communications, such as the outsourcing newsletter can help to explain changes, and tell staff about amendments to the operation of the agreement. If those amendments result from suggestions by specific staff members or teams, then make sure that the readers know this! In Chapter 12 we offer a number of ideas for improving the communication within the LIS itself and, of course, to the customers and the suppliers.

Communications between staff and supplier

Improved communications with your supplier will also help everyone to cope. Are there regular meetings with the supplier to monitor progress? Perhaps staff members, besides the negotiating team, can be observers at the meetings and take responsibility for telling their colleagues what happened there. A front-line staff member could speak up for the interests of LIS clients, and in doing so get to know the supplier's team better.

Business planning

Business planning skills can be used to ensure that the problems are kept to a minimum. Proper project plans will highlight the critical dates when reports or meetings are due, and when information about how things are going can be exchanged between the parties. Staff can collect details of problems and successes that can go onto the agenda of the regular checkpoint meetings. Staff may need to be trained for some of these roles, which again can be presented as a positive outcome from the changes.

Marketing the service

Staff can be involved in marketing the new services and being advocates for the changes. To do this they will need the sort of understanding that comes with being closely involved with the outsourcing development or operation process, which should lead to an understanding not only of where the difficulties lie but of possible ways to resolve them.

Involving staff representatives

Enlist your allies in the process of coping with your staff's natural disquiet at some of these changes. Keep the staff representatives (whether from a trades union or a staff association) involved in the changes, and attempt to deal openly and honestly with objections and fears. There may be a simple answer, or it may just be something that nobody has yet thought of, so consider each comment carefully. But you may need to be firm about the path that the LIS needs to follow, no matter how sympathetically you receive the representatives.

Above all, keep the channels of communication open and continuously engaged. Remember one thing – management actions often speak louder than words. If you tell staff that all is well but act as if the LIS is under constant threat from an aggressive or predatory partner, they will act accordingly.

Opportunities for all

Sometimes there are opportunities to show the staff that there is a very positive side to having an outsourced service. They may be able to acquire new skills in managing such a project. It will give staff and others the opportunity for self-analysis and to focus on being more accountable. Likewise it will offer staff, perhaps for the first time, the opportunity to see the 'bigger picture' in how the LIS functions, and links together with other parts of the organization and the outside world. Other opportunities may occur in that staff can learn new skills such as facilitator/teaching roles. There could be a shift in type of jobs available, for example more IT posts, project management and staff management.

The LIS manager will need to be constantly aware of the opportunities to 'sell' the outsourcing idea to staff so that they take up a positive view of how it will affect the LIS.

Summary

In this chapter, we have seen that staff have legitimate concerns about what happens to them when outsourced services are introduced, and that it is often the front-line staff who have to take action to resolve difficulties between the LIS, customers and suppliers. It is possible for management to take some positive steps to deal with the situation:

- Do not tire of explaining what is happening, and of putting fears to rest.
- Use as many channels of communication as you can.
- Be open with staff and show them what is going on.
- Be true to your words in your own relationships with staff, suppliers and customers.

12

Communication strategies

In this chapter we remind you of:

- the importance of a communication strategy
- the tools for your communications with staff and customers
- getting the message clear
- ways to avoid conflict.

The importance of a communication strategy

Outsourcing is often a traumatic event in an organization's history, so it is not surprising that it is frequently accompanied by a lack of understanding, deliberate or otherwise, on the part of some sectors of your community. It's important therefore that you devise an effective communication strategy to tell people what is going on and to set their fears aside.

It's a good time to raise your communications profile in the organization or community because something is so obviously changing in its midst. Discussing the changes gives you an opportunity to invite comment. Do the changes, in fact, meet everyone's requirements? If not, what else is needed? If the outsourcer is offering services that have not been provided before, what are they and how do people get the best out of them? Members of your organization will be interested in these new services. Suddenly this is positive change, and there is a good story to tell that focuses on the LIS.

The tools for your communications with staff and customers

There is a range of channels that you can use to communicate your message to your users. Depending on your situation you will have access to some or all of them, but you will always have scope to employ some of them, because they do not depend on being able to call on expensive electronic media, or anything other than some of your working time.

Publications

You can use your own publications or somebody else's to get your message across! Your own might include leaflets or more ambitious and expensive brochures to tell people about the services that you offer, and about your outsourcing partners. Often the partner is anxious for the client's staff to know more about the services on offer (it may after all create additional business) and your outsourcer may therefore help with the communications effort, either with information or even with funding. You would be quite brave to decide to have an 'outsourcing newsletter', but if there is a lot of anxiety it might be the way to face this head-on. If you have a general LIS newsletter, there is scope for information to be included on a regular basis. People want to know what is happening, and that there is something in it for them. Remind them!

If there is an internal newspaper or newsletter you have a different opportunity to get the message across. This time it will be different from your own publicity – and there is no reason why you should not do both – because the internal news will be viewed as independent of your own operation. Ensure that you are able to inspect the copy before it goes to press: you will be able to correct journalistic licence, and ensure that there is a positive and intelligent message in the story that goes beyond 'the library contains books'.

The intranet

Your intranet can be an excellent means of getting across information about the services offered by the LIS and the supplier, not least because of the ability to link directly to those services either somewhere else on the intranet or on the supplier's website. Don't underestimate the problems you may have in linking outside the organization, especially if your IT department includes software that restricts the range of available websites, or doesn't provide internet access at all.

If you have web-editing software such as FrontPage on hand, you can quickly create pages that give information on current events and situations, so you can have relevant copy on the day that important changes happen. You can obtain very reliable free web-editing software, which you can run on a standalone if your network does not support it. Many of the software products use templates rather than asking you to design from scratch, so you don't need to be a design genius to produce good results. Alternatively, many content management systems now allow you to type in a story and generate a full intranet page from the text.

Personal contact

Use the opportunities offered by your personal contacts, and those of your staff, to spread the news about what you are doing in the LIS. Whether talking in an informal environment like the lunch queue, or engaging your customers in conversation when they visit the LIS, there are plenty of chances to tell customers personally what is changing and why. This approach will also make it easier for your customers to discuss their concerns with you when the outsourcing agreement is under way, since you and your team will have made yourselves that much more approachable.

Presentations

If there are concerns, they will be better dealt with by going to the users and talking to them than by sending them a stream of leaflets. A presentation should be an interaction between the speaker and the audience rather than a monologue. If there are already regular presentations by the LIS team, then information about outsourcing can be included in those talks. If there are no presentations, this may be the time to consider starting them. Whichever way, there is a good opportunity to reinforce the position of the LIS in the organization, and to explain how the outsourcing agreement makes this an even stronger position. You could invite any members of LIS staff who remain uncertain about the arrangements, as a means of reassuring them too.

Training sessions

Make sure that your customers know the right way to make use of services – for example that they do not make systematic infringements of copyright law when they use your electronic collection. A slot on the induction course run by your organization will allow you to introduce the concept of an outsourced service to new members of the community – and newcomers to your environment may well be more used to outsourcing than people who have been with you for a long time. For the long-established people, run sessions that explain how to obtain services and allay concerns that somehow outsourcing parts of the service amounts to dismantling the entire LIS.

Regular meetings

Hold regular meetings with users and with your suppliers in the outsourced environment, especially if you have already published standards of service. These meetings form an important part of your communications strategy for the outsourced service. Make sure they take place, and that people recognize the opportunity they present. Even if only a few people are there, they will take your message away with them.

Open days

Holding an open day has the potential to interfere with the normal running of the LIS, but it may well bring in new customers. The supplier may help organize an open day: you should ask it to send representatives to talk to customers, and perhaps make some presentations of the services. The supplier may have some freebies that can be handed out to visitors, which will remind them of the LIS for some time to come. Try to get the supplier to give you something that will be around for some time. Pens and paper are nice but they run out and get thrown away: stress busters and executive toys hang around longer.

Getting the message clear

Whichever method or methods you use, make sure that the message is clear. LIS professionals tend to use jargon and acronyms, but you need to cut through this to tell people how the system works. Try to get your supplier to do the same. If you need to use technical terms, explain what they mean in lay language: 'SDI' still means an American defence system to many people, while 'alerting service' could mean someone who takes your phone calls and sends you a summary in the manner of a business agency. If you need to use a technical term, make sure the reader or listener knows what it means, and doesn't feel annoyed that you won't share what you know.

Ways of avoiding conflict

Open communication along the lines discussed here is the way to ensure that problems are dealt with early, and do not become major issues. Use your skills to detect problems in meetings: look for signs that people are upset or awkward about something, and try to get the chair to invite them to air any problems. Body language, if you are good at reading it, will tell you a lot about how someone feels about a proposal or the subject under discussion. Otherwise you may have to resort to having agenda items that reflect known concerns, and hoping that this will flush out the biggest difficulties.

Summary

This chapter has looked at the issues of communications, and shown the benefits of having a communications strategy for your outsourcing programme. We have discussed the main tools that organizations and communities use to communicate on a range of issues, and recommend these to you as means of getting your message across. Finally, we looked briefly at how to reduce conflict over your outsourced service, and how to bring out potential difficulties by sensing the discomfort of your customer representatives and encouraging them to express their concerns.

Bibliography

The URLs of the websites included in this bibliography were correct at the time of writing in late 2004.

Chapter 1   LIS outsourcing: an introduction

American Library Association (2003) *Outsourcing and Privatization*, ALA, www.ala.org/ala/ourassociation/governingdocs/aheadto2010/outsourcing.htm.

Ball, David and Earl, Carleton (2002) Outsourcing and Externalization: current practice in UK libraries, museums and archives, *Journal of Librarianship and Information Science,* **34** (4), (December), 197–206.

Ball, David (2003) A Weighted Decision Matrix for Outsourcing Library Services, *The Bottom Line: Managing Library Finances,* **16** (1), 25–30.

Boss, R. W. (1999) Guide to Outsourcing in Libraries, *Library Technology Reports,* **34** (5), 559–680.

Burge, Suzanne (1998) *Much Pain, Little Gain: privatisation and UK government libraries.* Paper presented at the 64th IFLA General Conference, Amsterdam, 16–21 August, www.ifla.org/ifla/IV/ifla64/187-139e.htm.

Dunk, Linda (2000) *Outsourcing and Externalization by Libraries, Museums and Archives: literature review*, London, CPI for Resource.

Ebbinghouse, Carol (2002) Library Outsourcing: a new look, *Searcher: The Magazine for Database Professionals*, **10** (4), 63–9, www.infotoday.com/searcher/apr02/ebbinghouse.htm.

Evers, Liesbeth (2001) ISPs Failing on Downtime Agreements, *IT Week*, (7 February), www.itweek.co.uk/News/1120755.

Great Britain. Cabinet Office (1991) *Competing for Quality/Buying Better Public Services* (Cm 1730), London, HMSO.

Intner, Sheila and Kamm, Sue (1997) Outsource Discourse, *American Libraries*, (October), 63–6.

Johnston, Janis L. (1996) Outsourcing: new name for an old practice, *Law Library Journal*, **88** (1), 128–34.

Jones, W. (1997) Outsourcing Basics, *Information Systems Management*, **14** (1), 66–9.
Sets out the components of a sound outsourcing evaluation. Covers: asking the right questions; knowing what outsourcing is; establishing sound reasons for outsourcing; weighing advantages and disadvantages; managing the people issues; using a competitive methodical approach; considering all stakeholders; understanding the vendors; negotiating a sound contract; encouraging user ownership of the outsourcing concept; managing the relationship with a retained team; and acting quickly.

Kemp, Alasdair (1994) Contracting Out Library and Information Services, Speaker: Ann Lawes, *Inform*, **162**, (March), 2–3.

Lawes, Ann (1994) Contracting Out, *New Library World*, **95** (1114), 8–12.
There is a strong general trend towards outsourcing specific functions in modern organizations, both in government and corporate libraries. Examines reasons why companies contract out together with the advantages and disadvantages. Examines who actually are the library and information contractors, specialist information

service companies, specialist suppliers, facilities management companies, management consultants and storage companies. Looks at the fundamental principles which should be adhered to, including: quality requirements and specification. Examines staffing and management issues, and relationships and benefits of permanent and temporary staff, and their employer. Managing of contract staff and communication is extremely important, as is staff development and training. Concludes that long-term social issues and their wide-ranging implications should be addressed.

Library of Congress (2003) *Online Newsletter of the Cataloging Directorate Library of Congress,* **11** (5), www.loc.gov/catdir/lccn/lccn1105.html.

Morton-Schwalb, Sandy (1997) The Ins and Outs of Outsourcing: the changing, evolving scene for information professionals, *Database*, (June/July), 41–2.

Naylor, Chris (2000a) Liverpool Scores with Supplier Selection, *Bookseller*, (2 June), 28–9.

Naylor, Chris (2000b) When the Supplier Selects, *Bookseller*, (18 February), 28–9.

Oder, Norman (1997) Outsourcing Model – or Mistake? The collection development controversy in Hawaii, *Library Journal*, **122** (5), 15.

    Facing a major budget crunch, the Hawaii State Public Library System awarded a five-and-a-half-year, $11.2 million contract to a vendor (Baker & Taylor) for collection development. Hawaii librarians argue that outsourcing sacrifices local expertise and a central part of their professional identity. Discusses the controversy from opposing points of view.

Ogburn, Joyce L. (1994) An Introduction to Outsourcing, *Library Acquisitions: Practice and Theory*, **18** (4), 363–6.

    Discusses the contracting out, by libraries, of technical services such as cataloguing to specialized commercial organizations (vendors). Considers outsourcing as a business strategy and looks briefly at the implications for acquisitions and collection development-ment. Concludes that, as with other business arrangements, preliminary steps before considering outsourcing, such as defining quality and the expectations of both parties, must be taken. Acquisitions librarians and collection development librarians have extensive experience with managing contracts with vendors but also have to think in new terms and develop new relationships, with vendor services expanding. Acquisitions librarians have many skills to offer in managing outsourcing arrangements, and general management and leadership abilities will still be necessary both for the staff working within the library and the contract services.

Ojala, M. (1996) Outsourcing or Ouch-sourcing?, *Library Manager*, (February), 29.

Looks at ways in which libraries can cope with the prospects of the outsourcing of some or all of their services. Highlights the need for awareness of the strengths and weaknesses of the library operation; paying attention to changing attitudes of people in the parent organization; and maintaining flexibility in management. Taking a proactive stance by outsourcing functions not within the library's core competencies will be seen as good management, and should forestall attempts at further inroads into services; however, such efforts need to be combined with promoting the subsequent increased efficiency to the clients.

Portugal, Frank (1997) *Exploring Outsourcing: case studies of corporate libraries*, Washington, DC, Special Libraries Association.

Renaud, Robert (1997) Learning to Compete: competition, outsourcing, and academic libraries, *The Journal of Academic Librarianship*, (March), 85–90.

Schneider, Anne (ed.) (1998) Outsourcing (Special issue), *The Bottom Line: Managing Library Finances*, **11** (3), 97–121.

Sweetland, James H. (2002) Outsourcing Library Technical Services: what we think we know, and don't know, *The Bottom Line:*

Managing Library Finances, **14** (3), 164–76.

White, Herbert S. (2000) Library Outsourcing and Contracting: cost-effectiveness or shell game?, *Library Journal,* **123** (11), 56–7, reprinted in: *Librarianship – Quo Vadis?,* Englewood, CO, Libraries Unlimited, 297–9.

Whitlatch, Jo Bell (2003) Reference Futures: outsourcing, the web, or knowledge counseling, *Reference Services Review,* **31** (1), 26–30.

Woodsworth, Anne (1998) Outsourcing: a tempest in a teapot, *Library Journal,* (1 March), 46.

Woodsworth, Anne and Williams, James F. II (1993) *Managing the Economics of Owning, Leasing and Contracting Out Information Services,* Burlington, VT/Aldershot, Ashgate.

Bibliographies

Canada. Canadian Heritage. Arts Policy Branch (2003) *Bibliography on Outsourcing in Heritage Institutions,* www.pch.gc.ca/progs/arts/pdf/out-bib/1_e.cfm (and linked pages).

Colver, Marylou and Wilson, Karen A. (eds) (1997) *Selected Annotated Bibliography: outsourcing library technical services operations,* 193–219, Chicago, IL, ALA.

Hirshon, Arnold and Winters, Barbara (1997) *Bibliography on Outsourcing*: outsourcing library technical services: how-to-do-it manual for librarians, 161–4, New York, Neal Schuman.

Johnson, Peggy (ed.) (1997) *Bibliography.* New Directions in Technical Services: trends and sources (1993–1995), Chicago, IL, ALA.

Websites

Relating to outsourcing issues in school libraries, museums and government
Chapman Tripp Barristers & Solicitors, New Zealand,

www.archive.org/web/20010513075105http://www.chapmantripp.
co.nz/publish/itoutsou.htm.

Chubb Insurance for Businesses, Museum Notes,
www.web.archive.org/web/19980515233610http://www.chubb.com/
library/notes97.html/outsourcing.

Education Network of Connecticut, http://csunet.ctstateu.edu/ednet/.

In the Ring, GovExec.com – Management,
www.govexec.com/features/0997s1.htm.

Museum Digital Library Collective, www.museumlicensing.org.

National Library of Australia, Gateways,
www.nla.gov.au/ntwkpubs/gw/31/31.html.

Smith Nightingale, Demetra and Pindus, Nancy (1997) *The Urban
Institute: privatization of public services – a background paper,*
www.urban.org/pubman/privitiz.html.

The Outsourcing Institute, New York, www.outsourcing.com.

General

Bigates Outsourcing (outsourcing articles in favour)
www.bigates.com/html/T_resource_links.htm.

Outsourcing Institute (claims to neutrality)
www.outsourcing.com/.

Library outsourcing articles
www.itcompany.com/inforetriever/adm_outs.htm.

Chapter 2   Be brutal: the information audit

Davenport, Thomas and Prusak, Laurence (1998) *Working Knowledge:
how organizations manage what they know,* Boston, Harvard Business
School Press.

Griffiths, Peter (2001) 'All That Glitters': the role of the information
professional in handling rogue information on the internet, *Online*

Information 2001: proceedings, Oxford, Learned Information, 17–23.

Griffiths, Peter (2004) Performing an Information Audit: identifying gaps and areas in need of development, *Content Management Focus,* **3** (4), 13–17.

Hyams, Elspeth (2001) Nursing the Evidence: the Royal College of Nursing information strategy, *Library Association Record,* **103** (12), 747–9.

Jones, Rebecca and Burwell, Bonnie (2004) Information Audits: building a critical process, *Searcher: The Magazine for Database Professionals,* **12** (1), 50–6.

Nielson, Jakob (1998) Reputation Managers are Happening, *Alertbox,* (5 September), www.useit.com/alertbox/990905.html.

Nielson, Jakob (1999) The Reputation Manager, *Alertbox,* (8 February), www.useit.com/alertbox/980208.html.

Pantry, Sheila (ed.) (1999), *Building Community Information Networks: strategies and experiences,* London, Library Association Publishing.

Pantry, Sheila and Griffiths, Peter (1998) *Becoming a Successful Intrapreneur: a practical guide to creating an innovative information service,* London, Library Association Publishing.

Pantry, Sheila and Griffiths, Peter (2000) *Developing a Successful Service Plan,* The Successful LIS Professional Series, London, Library Association Publishing.

Pantry, Sheila and Griffiths, Peter (2001) *The Complete Guide to Preparing and Implementing Service Level Agreements,* 2nd edn, London, Library Association Publishing.

Pantry, Sheila and Griffiths, Peter (2002) *Creating a Successful e-Information Service,* London, Facet Publishing.

Pantry, Sheila, and Griffiths, Peter (2003) *Your Essential Guide to Career Success,* 2nd edn, London, Facet Publishing; Lanham, MD, Scarecrow Press.

Yeates, Robin (2003) *Reputation Management for Libraries: overcoming reluctance to collaborate.* Paper presented at Interlend 2003: Breaking

barriers, New Hall, Cambridge, July 2003,
www.cilip.org.uk/groups/fil/c2003k.rtf.

Facet Publishing (formerly Library Association Publishing) books are
available from Bookpoint Ltd, Mail Order Department, 39 Milton
Park, Abingdon, Oxon OX14 4SB. Tel: +44 (0)1235 400400; Fax:
+44 (0)1235 400454; e-mail: facet@bookpoint.co.uk.
For information and direct ordering see: www.facetpublishing.co.uk.
Further information also available from:
www.sheilapantry.com/books; e-mail: sp@sheilapantry.com.

Chapter 3 When to outsource: using the results of the information audit

Agada, John (1997) Information Counseling and the Outsourcing
Challenge to Corporate Librarianship, *College & Research Libraries*,
58 (4), 338–47.

Assinder, Debbie (2004) Delivering Business Services for Libraries,
Library and Information Update, **3** (3), 32–4.

Ball, David and Earl, Carleton (2002) Outsourcing and Externalisation:
current practice in UK libraries, museums and archives, *Journal of
Librarianship and Information Science,* **34** (4), 197–206.

Beaumont, Nicholas and Costa, Christina (2003) Information
Technology Outsourcing in Australia. In *Advanced Topics in
Information Resources Management*, Hershey, PA, Idea Group, 192–219.

Burge, Suzanne (1998) *Much Pain, Little Gain: privatisation and UK government libraries*. Paper presented at the 64th IFLA General
Conference, Amsterdam, 16–21 August,
www.ifla.org/IV/ifla64/187–139e.htm.

Bush, Carmel C. et al. (1994) Toward a New World Order: a survey of
outsourcing capabilities of vendors for acquisitions, cataloging and
collection development services, *Library Acquisitions*: *Practice and
Theory*, **18** (4), 397–416.

Business 360 (2003) *Business Research Outsourcing: experience, lessons and opinions: summary results of a survey conducted by Business 360 in partnership with TFPL*, www.business360.com/ebic/survey1.asp.
The survey is to be updated each year in connection with the European Business Information Conference, which is usually held in March.

Business Insight (2003) *First Steps to Outsourcing Business Information for Libraries*, Birmingham,
www.birmingham.gov.uk/Media/Library%20Outsourcing.PDF?
MEDIA_ID=53628&FILENAME=Library%20Outsourcing.PDF.

Calabrese, Alice and Wozny, Jay (1995) The CLS Bottom Line: it's more than money, it's service (Chicago Library System), *The Bottom Line: Managing Library Finances,* **8** (2),18–22.

Canadian Bar Association (1996) Privatization of Government Services: understanding the process & the opportunities [papers presented at the 21st annual Institute on Continuing Legal Education, Tuesday June 4, 1996, The Westin Harbor Castle, Toronto, Ontario Branch.

Collins, J. S. and Millen, R. A. (1995) Information Systems Outsourcing by Large American Industrial Firms: choices and impacts, *Information Resources Management Journal,* **8** (1), 5–13
A survey was mailed to the chief information officers of the 500 largest industrial firms in the USA to investigate outsourcing of information systems. The results from the 110 responses indicate the extent and effects of outsourcing among users of such services. The survey also collected data about the outsourcing plans of non-users. The survey provided information about the planning and implementation issues encountered, benefits achieved, and impact on performance. This study is a benchmark of current outsourcing practice. In addition, it tests some commonly accepted assumptions about the reasons for outsourcing, and the effects of outsourcing on the firm.

Coopers & Lybrand (1996) *Valuing the Economic Costs and Benefits of Libraries*,Wellington, New Zealand Library & Information Association.

Coulter, Jane (ed.) (1994) *Doing More With Less? Contracting out and efficiency in the public sector*, PSRC Collected Papers 1, Public Sector Research Centre, Sydney, University of New South Wales.

Cram, Jennifer (1995) *Moving from Cost Centre to Profitable Investment: managing the perception of a library's worth*. Paper presented at Asia–Pacific Library Conference, Brisbane, 28 May–1 June 1995, Australasian Public Libraries and Information Services, (September), 107–13.

Crismond, Linda A. (1994) Outsourcing from the A/V Vendor's Viewpoint: the dynamics of a new relationship, *Library Acquisitions: Practice and Theory*, **18** (4), 375–81.

Cronk, J. and Sharp, J. (1995) A Framework for Deciding what to Outsource in Information Technology, *Journal of Information Technology*, **10** (4), 259–67.
Contribution to a special issue devoted to outsourcing information systems. Examines the theory and background of outsourcing from a general perspective. A strategic framework should be developed to make it possible to determine which information technologies activities should be outsourced and which should be obtained internally.

Currie, W. L. (1996) Outsourcing in the Private and Public Sectors: an unpredictable IT strategy, *European Journal of Information Systems*, **4** (4), 226–36.
Considers the literature on information technology outsourcing in both private and public sector British and American organizations. Introduces the results from a questionnaire survey of 200 UK private and public sector organizations on information technology outsourcing. Looks at the proportion of organizations that use outsourcing, how contracts are negotiated and the type of information

technology solutions preferred by information technology managers.

Dwyer, Jim (1994) Does Outsourcing Mean You're Out? *Technicalities*, **14** (6), 1, 6.

Evans, John E. (1995) Cost Analysis of Public Services in Academic Libraries (abbreviated version of author's doctoral thesis), *Journal of Interlibrary Loan, Document Delivery & Information*, **5** (3), 27–70.

Harrington, Keith (2003) Contracting Out of a Public Library Service: business to be, or not to be?, *Library Management*, **24** (4), 187–92.

Hill, Janet Swan (1998) Boo! Outsourcing from the Cataloging Perspective, *The Bottom Line: Managing Library Finances,* **11** (3), 116–21.

Intner, Sheila S. (1994) Outsourcing: what does it mean for technical services?, *Technicalities*, **14** (3), 3–5.

Martin, Murray S. (1995) Outsourcing: implication that the private sector can provide many services more economically than the public sector, *The Bottom Line: Managing Library Finances*, **8** (1), 28–30.

Mielke, Linda (1990) Cost Finding: why it is important (per unit costs for a specific service, e.g., adding gift books to your collection), *Public Libraries*, **29**, (September/October), 282–8.

Mielke, Laurie R. (1991) Sermon on the Amount: costing out children's services. Revision of paper presented at the ALA Conference, June 1990, *Public Libraries*, (September/October), 279–82.

Nichols, John V. (1993) Cost Sharing and Public Libraries. In *Against all Odds*, Fort Atkinson, WI, Highsmith Press, 29–41.

Raiders of the Lost Jobs (1998) *Public Employee*, (January/February), 6–9.

Robinson, Barbara M. (1990) Costing Question Handling and ILL/Photocopying: a study of two state contract libraries, *The Bottom Line: Managing Library Finances*, (Summer), 20–5.

Rosenberg, Philip (1992) *Elements of Cost*, Keeping the Book, Fort Atkinson, WI, Highsmith Press, 431–9.

US Bureau of the Budget (1955) *Bulletin 55–4* (issued 15 January 1955), Washington DC, The Bureau.

White, Herbert S. (1998) Library Outsourcing and Contracting: cost-effectiveness or shell game?, *Library Journal*, **123** (11), 56–7, reprinted in *Librarianship – Quo Vadis?* Englewood, CO, Libraries Unlimited, 297–9.

Websites

Business Insight
www.birmingham.gov.uk/businessinsight.bcc.

Freshminds
www.freshminds.com/.

PUBSIG-L, a discussion list for issues relating to New Zealand public libraries
wwwlists.ccc.govt.nz/archives/pubsig-l.html.

Chapter 4 Information ownership and using an information service provider

Block, Rick J. (1994) Cataloging Outsourcing: issues and options (at Tufts University), *Serials Review*, **20** (3), 73–7.

Brockhurst, Christina J. (1993) Pay and Terms Rule Hits 'Testing' Plans (EC Directive Affects Compulsory Competitive Tendering Process), *Library Association Record*, (January), 19.

European Communities. Commission (2003) *Amended Proposal for a Directive of the European Parliament and of the Council on the Re-use and Commercial Exploitation of Public Sector Information*, ftp://ftp.cordis.lu/pub/econtent/docs/acte_en_greffe_2000_final.pdf and also available in other EU official languages from links on www.cordis.lu/econtent/psi/psi_policy.htm.

Matthews, Joseph R. (2002) *Internet Outsourcing Using an Application*

Service Provider: a how-to-do-it manual for librarians, New York, Neal-Schuman.

Collecting societies

Copyright Licensing Agency
www.cla.co.uk.
Educational Recording Agency
www.era.org.uk.
Newspaper Licensing Agency
www.nla.co.uk.

Chapter 5   How to outsource

Agnew, Grace (1993) Contracting for Technical Services: shelf-ready services for books. In Crismod, L. F. (ed.), *Case Studies on Library Financial Management*, Fort Atkinson, WI, Highsmith Press.

Alvestrand, Viveka (2004) British Library Rolls Out Bespoke Research Service, *Information World Review*, www.iwr.co.uk/iwreview/1152017.

American Council on Excellence. Center for Institutional and International Initiatives. Academic Excellence and Cost Management National Awards Program (2002) *The Washington Research Library Consortium: outsourcing to ourselves*, www.acenet.edu/programs/cost–awards/readAbstract.cfm?awardID =65.

Anderson, A. J. et al. (1998) Farming out the Library, *Library Journal*, **123** (14), 153–5.

Association for Library Collections and Technical Services. Reproduction of Library Materials Section. Subcommittee on Contract Negotiations for Commercial Reproductions of Library and Archival Materials (1994) Contract Negotiations for the Commercial Microform Publishing of Library and Archival

Materials: guidelines for librarians and archivists, *Library Resources & Technical Services*, (January), 72–85.

Baker & Taylor (1998) *Outsourcing: opportunity or not* (prepared for ALA Outsourcing Task Force), January.

Barnes, James B. (1995) Outsourcing: is it in your association's future? *American Society of Association Executives*, 20008, 1 April.

Beaumont and Associates Inc. (1995) *Library Technical Services Study: final report* (prepared for the Metro Task Force on Cost Savings through Cooperative Activities).

Bénaud, Claire-Lise and Bordeianu, Sever (1998) *Outsourcing Library Operations in Academic Libraries: an overview of issues and outcomes*, Littleton, CO, Libraries Unlimited.

Designed to give librarians a broad understanding of outsourcing issues in academic libraries. Synthesizes prevailing theories on the topic and describes current outsourcing practices in all areas of librarianship. After a historical overview and a detailed analysis of the pros and cons of outsourcing, the authors outline the steps for planning and implementing a successful outsourcing programme. Individual chapters cover collection development, acquisitions and serials management, cataloguing, retrospective conversion, authority control, preservation, and public services and systems. A special feature of the book is a detailed survey of more than 200 academic research libraries and other academic libraries on outsourcing practices. Claire-Lise Bénaud is Head, Cataloging Department, University of New Mexico, Albuquerque and Sever Bordeianu is Head, Serials Cataloging, General Library, at the same library.

Block, Rick J. (1994) Cataloging Outsourcing: issues and options, *Serials Review*, **20** (3), 73–7.

Bush, Carmel et al. (1994) Toward a New World Order: a survey of outsourcing capabilities of vendors for acquisitions, cataloging and collection development services, *Library Acquisitions: Practice & Theory*, **18** (4), 397–414.

Article included in a special section on outsourcing (contracting out). A survey of selected library materials jobbers, cataloguing agents and library consortia shows that communication standards, vendor and library automation, and a new partnership between vendors and libraries are leading to greater opportunities for outsourcing acquisitions, cataloguing and collection development. Currently libraries can depend upon vendors for preorder searching, verification and claiming functions, as well as copy and original cataloguing. Libraries can receive shelf-ready materials from jobbers or cataloguing agents; and those that collect mainstream materials have the most options; others must shop among vendors. Collection development is the function least changed by automation, but materials jobbers are orienting more electronic services towards this area. Concludes that librarians should become full partners in the development of contract services and, to do this, they must understand the evolving roles of the traditional partners and the costs and risks involved.

Cann Casciato, Daniel (1994) Tepid Water for Everyone? The future OLUC, catalogers, and outsourcing (online union catalog), *OCLC Systems & Services*, **10**, (Spring), 5–8.

Carpenter, Kenneth E. and Carr, Jane (1990) Microform Publishing Contracts, *Microform Review*, **19**, (Spring), 83–100.

Chester, Wendy (1997) *Outsourcing – Ready or Not?* A discussion paper presented at a seminar on outsourcing library technical services, organized by the Public Libraries Branch at the State Library of New South Wales on 4 August, www.slnsw.gov.au/plb/confer/outsrc/costword.htm.

Christmas, Gary M. (1998) *Riverside County Library System: contract evolution* (prepared for ALA Outsourcing Task Force), January.

CILIP, *Buyer's Guide*, www.cilip.org.uk/buyersguide/index.html.

Clouston, J. S. (1996) The Shelf-ready Book: outsourcing from a public services and administrative perspective, *Taking Stock: Libraries and the Book Trade*, **5** (1), 11–16.

Examines the issue of outsourcing to obtain the shelf-ready book from the aspect of public services and the viewpoint of a library administrator. Questions the necessity of having totally in-house cataloguing. Highlights the advantages of having outside cataloguing and supplementary services. Outsourcing should not replace cataloguing departments but be dependent on circumstances. The main reasons for its implementation should be improved services rather than financial savings.

College & Research Libraries News (1995) University of Alberta outsources cataloging, **56** (3), 140.

Colver, Marylou and Wilson, Karen (eds) (1997) *Outsourcing Technical Services Operations*, Chicago, IL, American Library Association.

County of Riverside. State of California (1997) Agreement with Library Systems and Services, LLC for Provision of County Library Services, (17 June).

Cowing, Sue (1994) State Public Library System Becoming Wal-Martisized, *The Honolulu Advertiser*, (9 February), B4.

Desmarais N. and Luther J. (1997) The Evolution from Physical to Virtual Library, *Against the Grain*, **8** (6), 24, 27.

Looks at developments that have led to a move towards the virtual library. Traces outsourcing developments in acquisitions and cataloguing, and the growth of access verses ownership of materials. The virtual library will lead to a self-service library where users bypass the librarian or the library entirely. The growing use of the internet by publishers will lead to a variety of pricing models for document delivery. The virtual library will shift the preservation function to the publisher and, as economics drives the shift towards electronic formats, the library may become a repository for information for the information underprivileged who cannot afford electronic access.

Diedrichs, C. P. (1996) Acquisitions Management in Changing Times,

Library Resources & Technical Services, **40** (3), 237–47, 50. Paper presented at the ALCTS Acquisitions Section Preconference (Business of Acquisitions), Chicago, 22–3, June 95.
Acquisitions managers are expected to cope with rapid changes affecting their work and become expert in new areas, including document delivery; copy cataloguing; outsourcing; and contract negotiation. New functions include: selection and downloading of catalogue records from bibliographic utilities at the preorder stage; completion of cataloguing on receipt where adequate copy exists and managing document delivery programmes that complement the traditional collection development process. Examines three concerns affecting acquisitions managers: the essential elements of change involved (external environment, organizational capability, understanding the change process, and how individuals will react to the change process); ways in which acquisitions managers can exhibit leadership in this environment, particularly with those who report to them; and how acquisitions librarians can cope with this change (self-assessment, stress). [The author may be contacted by electronic mail at diedrichs.1@osu.edu.]

Diedrichs, Carol Pitts (1998) Using Automation in Technical Services to Foster Innovation: outsourcing, OCLC's Passport and PromptCat, *Journal of Academic Librarianship*, **24** (2), 113–120.

Dinerman, Gloria (1997) The Angst of Outsourcing, *Information Outlook*, **1** (4), 21–4.

Distad, Brian (1995) The Client Still Ranks First in U. Alberta Library's Restructuring, *Library Acquisitions: Practice & Theory*, **19** (4), 435–8.

Dixon, Catherine and Bordonaro, Frances G. (1997) Selection to Shelf: outsourcing book selection, copy cataloging, and physical processing at Fort Worth Public Library, *Outsourcing Library Technical Services Operations*, Chicago, IL, ALA, 137–53.

Dow, Ronald F. (1994) Sustaining Organization Advantage in Times of Financial Uncertainty: the context for research and development investments by academic libraries, *Library Trends*, **42** (3), 460–6.

Dubberley, Ronald A. (1998) Why Outsourcing is Our Friend, *American Libraries*, (January), 72–4.

Dudley, Martin P. (1994) Hertfordshire: franchising library services, *Public Library Journal*, (July/August), 98–9.

Dunkle, Clare B. (1996) Outsourcing the Catalog Department: a meditation inspired by the business and library literature, *Journal of Academic Librarianship*, (January), 33–44.

Contains a great number of insights into our role in the library organization and what makes or breaks an outsourcing operation. However, it is not entirely favourable to outsourcing. If anything, it is critical of the movement, arguing that in many cases it is done for the wrong reasons and without the research or back-up needed to make the operation successful.

Dunsire, Gordon (1992) Behind the Screens: needs of competitive tendering will encourage the use of standard machine readable catalog records, *Scottish Libraries*, (November/December), 6.

Duranceau, Ellen (1994) Vendor and Librarians Speak on Outsourcing, Cataloging, and Acquisitions, *Serials Review*, (Fall), 69–83.

Dwyer, James R. (1996) From PromptCat to Recat: or, you only catalog twice, *Technicalities*, (July/August), 14–15.

Eberhart G. et al. (1997) ALA's Midwinter Return to Washington, *American Libraries*, **28** (4), 66–71. Reports on the ALA's 1997 Midwinter Meeting, held 14–20 February, Washington, DC. Topics included internet access for children, outsourcing, internet filtering software, how to make libraries politically effective, and re-engineering the library industry to confront the risks and opportunities of the digital age.

Eddison, Betty (1997) Our Profession is Changing – Whether We Like It or Not, *Online*, **21** (1), 72–81.

Discusses outsourcing in the information industry. Highlights include information technology; special libraries; outsourcing in

Australia; public librarians; benchmarking and quality control; online searching; and outsourcing as a threat to information professionals.

Edmonds, Diana J. (1995) Instant Library – an Aladdin's Cave of Information Services, *The Law Librarian*, (September), 442–5.

Eisenberg, Mike and Repman, Judi (1997) The Sky is Falling, the Sky is Falling . . . or is it?, *Technology Connection*, **4** (3), (May–June), 20–1. Discusses the Hawaii State Public Library system decision to outsource library book selection to a vendor. Highlights include problems with the current contract, including lack of input from local librarians; and possible benefits of outsourcing, including the chance of having an outsourced baseline collection with discretionary funds for local purchases.

El-Sherbini, Magda (1995) Contract Cataloging: a pilot project for outsourcing Slavic books, *Cataloging & Classification Quarterly*, **20** (3), 57–73.

El-Sherbini, Magda (2002) Outsourcing of Slavic Cataloguing at the Ohio State University Libraries: evaluation and cost analysis, *Library Management*, **23** (6), 325–9.

Farmanfarmaian, Roxane (1996) B&T, Local Wholesaler Chooses Books for Hawaii Libraries, *Publishers Weekly*, (14 October), 15.

Farmanfarmaian, Roxane (1997) Hawaii Libraries vs. Baker & Taylor: Better Times Ahead?, *Publishers Weekly*, (3 March), 16.

Fast, Barry (1995) Outsourcing and PromptCat: OCLC service delivers cataloged books and updated holdings records, *Against the Grain*, (April), 50.

Field, Tom (1997) Caveat Emptor: an outsourcing buyers guide, *CIO*, **10** (12), 47–58.

Fischl, I. (1996) Outsourcing: a new management tool or just a fad?, *FID News Bulletin*, **46** (5), 171–3. Contribution to part 2 of a special issue on corporate information management: strategic information management in business and industry. Paper presented at the annual conference of the American Society for Information Science in Chicago, IL, 9–12 October 1995 on 'Reinventing Information Services: linking information services to business strategies' and first published in *Bulletin of the American Society for Information Science*, April/May 1996.

Defines outsourcing and its mechanisms, looks at historical developments leading to outsourcing, and considers the implications for and its impact on information services. Instead of considering outsourcing as a threat or just a way of cutting costs and eliminating services, if used in a sophisticated manner, it can become a strategic business tool.

Freeman, Gretchen (1998) Criteria for Automation Outsourcing (original work presented to ALA Outsourcing Task Force), 12 January.

Gerhardt, Lillian (1994) Editorial, The Hawaiian Punch: or – can a drip turn into a tidal wave?, *School Library Journal*, (February), 5.

Germain, Marc and Lorius, Marion (2000) Architectures des bibliothèques municipales à vocation régionale, *Bulletin des bibliothécaires de France*, **45** (3), 39–48, bbf.enssib.fr/bbf/html/2000_45_3 /2000-3-p39-lorius.xml.asp. While mainly concerned with the architectural aspects of these dozen or so major library building projects, the text also explains the context of the BMVR initiative.

Gershenfeld, Nancy (1994) Outsourcing Serials Activity at the Microsoft Corporation, *Serials Review*, **20** (3), 81–3.

Glasgow City Council (1999) *Glasgow City Council Libraries and Archives Best Value Service Review: public consultation paper*, www.glasgow.gov.uk/html/council/dept/cls/librev/librev.pdf.

Glick, Bryan (2004) Does your Outsourcing Agreement Measure Up? *Computing*, (27 March), www.vnunet.com/features/1153857.

Goede, Darryl (1993) *Marketing and Funds Development: a kit for Alberta public libraries*, APLMIT Committee, Edmonton, Alberta, Canada.

Gorman, Michael (1996) The Corruption of Cataloging, *Library Journal*, (15 September), 32–4.

Griffith, C. (1997) Law Librarians Embrace Change, *Information Today*, **14** (6), 18–19.

Considers how information technology is affecting the work of law librarians. Outsourcing is only one of the latest moves in law library management threatening the profession. Smaller or medium-sized law offices currently staffing a law library with a full-time professional are reviewing whether or not they continue to staff the position. Discusses the roles of management information systems professionals and law librarians.

Grupe, F. H. (1997) Outsourcing the Help Desk Function, *Information Systems Management*, **14** (2), 15–22.

Cost, performance, and service demands are driving organizations to outsource all or part of their help-desk functions. Selecting an appropriate vendor and preparing a detailed contract are key to forming a cost-effective and productive relationship that gives both the organization and the vendor a competitive advantage. Sets out a six-step approach that helps information systems managers delineate the goals, requirements, and terms on which such a relationship is based.

Guy, Robin Frederick (1993) Cataloguers Face Up to CCT Threat, CIGS seminar in Glasgow, February 1993, *Library Association Record*, (June), 366.

Hallman, Philip (1995) Outsourcing Media, *Against the Grain*, (September), 92–4 .

Halvey, John K. and Melby, Barbara Murphy (1996) *Information Technology Outsourcing Transactions: process, strategies, and contracts*, Chichester, John Wiley & Sons. Cumulative Supplements, 1999 and 2001.

Hamilton, William (1996) Focus Sections, Latest Books about Hawaii and the Public? You won't find them at state public libraries, *The*

Honolulu Advertiser, (10 November), B1, B4.

Harken, S. E. (1996) Outsourcing: ready, set, go? A cataloger's perspective, *Cataloging & Classification Quarterly*, **23** (2), 67–87. Considers the issues involved in outsourcing library cataloguing, including: the need to have dependable, good quality, records available to outsource; suitable vendors; librarians able to communicate their needs; and a means of acquiring bibliographic records and processing relatively easily, at a reasonable price. Describes the experiences of the Fritz Library, North Dakota University in using PALS, an online system based on OCLC MARC, and outlines the pitfalls to be avoided for successful outsourcing. The author may be contacted by electronic mail at Harken@plains.nodak.edu. Copies of this article can be obtained from the Haworth Document Delivery Service, Haworth Press, Inc., 10 Alice Street, Binghamton, New York, 13904–1580, USA. E-mail: getinfo@haworth.com.

Hatfield, Deborah (1994) Partnerships in Information Services: the contract library, *Special Libraries*, (Spring), 77–80.

Hawaii Will Counter B&T Suit: major monetary claim expected (1997) *Library Hotline*, (24 November), 2–3.

Helfer, Doris Small (1997) Insourced or Outsourced: a tale of two libraries, *Searcher: The Magazine for Database Professionals*, **5** (8), 68–70. Discussion of outsourcing library operations highlights two examples: (1) the Riverside County, CA, which had been outsourcing library operations to the City of Riverside, and switched to a private vendor; and (2) the Sun Microsystems Library which had operated as an outsourced library and recently decided to insource its library personnel.

Helfer, Doris Small (1998) Outsourcing, Teaming and Special Libraries: threats and opportunities, *Information Outlook*, (December), www.sla.org/pubs/serial/io/1998/dec98/helfer.html.

Hill, Cindy (1998) Insourcing the Outsourced Library: the Sun story, *Library Journal*, (1 March), 46–8.

Hill, Janet Swan (1998) Boo! Outsourcing from the Cataloguing Perspective, *Bottom Line: Managing Library Finances*, **11** (3), 116–21.

Hirshon, Arnold and Winters, Barbara (1996) *Outsourcing Library Technical Services: a how-to-do-it manual*, New York, Neal-Schuman. This book provides practical advice on how to: determine when outsourcing is an appropriate management tool in the process of re-engineering library technical services; conduct cost studies to evaluate technical operations; prepare formal requests-for-proposals to outsource the acquisition of books and periodicals, and for cataloguing; evaluate vendor responses and services; and monitor the quality of outsourced operations.

Hixon, B. (1997) Outsourcing the Electronic Library, *Managing Information*, **4** (6), 40–1. The Paul Hamlyn Learning Resource Centre (LRC) opened in Slough in September 1996, the third LRC to be opened by Thames Valley University. When it became clear in the early stages of the project that there were going to be problems in providing this comprehensive service with existing staff and that the University could not afford to fully equip the centre with the necessary technology, the provision of these services in the new LRC was offered to tender. Describes the provision of these services by International Computers Limited.

Hyams, Elspeth (2002) Bringing Glamour to Glasgow, *Library and Information Update*, (November), www.cilip.org.uk/update/issues/nov02/article2nov.html.

Newcastle City Council (2003a) *Libraries Set for £27m Investment* (news release, 27 November), www.newcastle.gov.uk/news.nsf/b8da7086f70880de8025677c002ee5 8d/3a6c83af8f88981f80256e630042d81d!OpenDocument.

Newcastle City Council (2003b) *Libraries and Information Service: PFI project* (Paper for Cabinet meeting, 31 October), www.newcastle-city-council.gov.uk/cab2003.nsf/57dc6634edbc 20fa80256ddd005cb069/0b8bb8d2f70e656a80256dc8005a0d78! OpenDocument.

Randall, Helen (2003) Library PFI/PPP in Higher Education: the legal context. In *Libraries with Oomph: PFI for higher education libraries: paper delivered at a seminar in London*, London, Nabarro Nathanson. Includes an overview of the procurement timetable and a review of library-specific issues. Available at www.nabarro.com/uploads/files/286.pdf.

Urquhart, Christine (2002) Applications of Outsourcing Theory to Collaborative Purchasing and Licensing. *VINE*, **32** (4), 63–70.

Chapter 6   What to include in your outsourcing agreement

Great Britain. Department of National Heritage (1997) *Reading the Future: a review of public libraries in England*, London, Department of National Heritage.

Investors in People UK (1996) *The Investors in People Standard*, London, Investors in People.

The Library Association (1992) *Framework for Continuing Professional Development* (and consultations for new framework), London, Library Association.

The Library Association (1995) *Model Statement of Standards for Public Library Services*, London, Library Association, www.cilip.org.uk/about/code.html.

The Library Corporation offers Fixed-fee Outsourcing Solution (1998) *Information Today*, (April), **15** (4), 57.

Chapter 7   Elements of the outsourcing agreement

Breaking News: LSSI under scrutiny in Fargo after bills overdue (2003) *Library Journal*, (15 August), www.libraryjournal.com/index.

Great Britain. Cabinet Office (1998) *Service First: the new charter programme*, London, Cabinet Office.

The Library Association (1999) *Code of Professional Conduct and Guidance Notes*, 3rd edn, London, Library Association (under revision).

Chapter 8   What the outsourcing agreement should look like

British Computer Society, *Industry Structure Model*, www.bcs.org/BCS/Products/Corporate/Industrymodel.

Great Britain. Department of National Heritage (1997) *Reading the Future: a review of public libraries in England*, London, Department of National Heritage.

Investors in People UK (1996) *The Investors in People Standard*, London, Investors in People.

The Library Association (1992) *Framework for Continuing Professional Development* (and consultations for new framework), London, Library Association, www.cilip.org.uk/qualifications/framework.html.

The Library Association (1995) *Model Statement of Standards for Public Library Services*, London, Library Association, www.cilip.org.uk/about/code.html.

Pantry, Sheila and Griffiths, Peter (2002) *Creating a Successful e-Information Service,* London, Facet Publishing; Lanham, MD, Scarecrow Press.

Chapter 9   Keeping the agreement on target

Audit Commission (1993) *Realising the Benefits of Competition: the client rôle for contracted services*, London, HMSO.

Brandt, Walter D. (1993) The Intelligence Bottleneck: too much sup-
ply – too little demand, *Journal of the Association for Global Strategic
Information*, **2** (2), 86–99. Cited in Clark, Pamela E. (1995) Client
Aspirations and Relationships: issues for the information manager.
In *New Roles, New Skills, New People*. Hatfield, University of
Hertfordshire Press, 9–31,
Discussion of the difficulties of establishing suitable performance
management systems for information services within the account-
ing regimes of many organisations.

Pantry, Sheila and Griffiths, Peter (2001) *The Complete Guide to
Preparing and Implementing Service Level* Agreements, 2nd edn,
London, Library Association Publishing.

Reuters Business Information (1995) *Information as an Asset: the invisible
goldmine*, Reuters Business Information.

Chapter 10 Keeping your users happy with the outsourced service

Kerr, George (1999) *Gaining and Retaining Customer Loyalty*, CPI occasional paper 3, West Lothian Council.

Sugg, Anne (ed.) (1998) *Consulting the Customer: using market research in
libraries. Proceedings of a seminar held at Stamford, Lincolnshire on 13th
October 1998*, Bruton, Capital Planning Information.

Thomas, Barbro (1996) *Contracting out of Public Libraries*. Paper presented at the 62nd IFLA General Conference, Guimaraes,
Portugal, 25–31 August, www.ifla.org/ifla/IV/ifla62/62-thob.htm.

Valauskas, Edward J. (1998) *A Review of Privatization*. Paper presented at
the 64th IFLA General Conference, Amsterdam, 16–21 August,
www.ifla.org/ifla/IV/ifla64/188-139e.htm.

Willett, Charles (1998) Consider the Source: a case against outsourcing
materials selection in academic libraries, *Collection Building*, **17** (2),
91–5.

Argues that outsourcing approval plans to vendors creates a preju-
dice against the alternative press. Business is guided by the
interests of corporate America and does not provide exposure to all
points of view. Argues that as the last truly free public space in
America, library managers have a duty to make alternative materials available for use and to secure the independence, integrity and
accountability of America's libraries.

Chapter 11 Keeping staff happy with the outsourced service

Bates, Mary Ellen (1997) Avoiding the Ax: how to keep from being
downsized or outsourced, *Information Outlook*, **1** (10), (October),
18–21.

Capital Planning Information (1998) *The Concept of Best Value: the impact
on library services: proceedings of a seminar held in September 1998*,
Bruton, CPI.

Capital Planning Information (1999) *Alternative Funding Streams For
Libraries: proceedings of a seminar held in April 1999*, Bruton, CPI.

Capital Planning Information (1999) *Best Value and Libraries: the reality
beckons?: proceedings of a seminar held in September 1999*, Bruton, CPI.

Capital Planning Information (1999) *Library Purchasing Consortia in the
UK: activity benefits and practice*, Bruton, CPI.

This major 180-page report, published by CPI on behalf of LIC as
Library and Information Commission Report No 16, is based on
research undertaken by Jo Pye and David Ball, of Bournemouth
University. The report provides an important, analytical review of
how purchasing consortia operate across the various library sectors
– public, higher education, further education, health.

Capital Planning Information (2001) *Outsourcing – Practice and
Opportunity in Libraries, Museums and Archives: proceedings of a seminar
held in March 2001*, Bruton, CPI.

Catalog Outsourcing: no clear-cut choice. Outsourcing library technical operation; practices in academic, public and special libraries.
Information Outlook, **1** (4), 21–4 (April 1997).

Cusworth, Marianne (1999) *The Future of Library and Information
Services: how Hertfordshire consulted in a best value context*, Bruton, CPI.

Dinerman, Gloria (1997) The Angst of Outsourcing, *Information
Outlook*, **1** (4), (April), 21–4.

Edmonds, Diana (1998) Facilities Management for Information
Services: outsourcing the impossible. In *Serials,* **11** (1), 219–22.

Goulding, A. et al. (1999) *Likely to Succeed: attitudes and aptitudes for an
effective information profession in the 21st century*, Library and
Information Commission research report 8,
www.lic.gov/publications/index.html.

Holt, Glen (1995) Catalog Outsourcing: no clear-cut choice, *Library
Journal*, **120** (15), (September), 34.

Jette, Karen D. and Clay-Edward, Dixon (1998) The
Outsourced/Contingent Workforce: abuse, threat, or blessing?,
Library Administration and Management, **12** (4), 220–5.

Kerr, George (1999) *Gaining and Retaining Customer Loyalty*, CPI occasional paper 3, West Lothian Council.

Liddle, David (1999) *Best Value: are libraries leading or following?*, Bruton,
CPI.

Outsourcing: special report (n.d.), www.vnunet.com/specials/1153874.

Schwalb, Sandy (1997) The Ins and Outs of Outsourcing: the changing, evolving scene for information professionals, *Database*, **20** (3),
41–2, 44–6
Examines the trend toward outsourcing in libraries and presents
views from information professionals in various work environments. Discussion covers privatization activities of government
agencies and libraries as well as corporate libraries, particularly law
firm libraries. The need for good library–vendor communication,

the effect on public libraries, and examples of both successful and problematic outsourcing are also highlighted.

TFPL Ltd (1999) *Skills for Knowledge Management: a briefing paper*, London, LIC. Executive summary and also full text at www.lic.gov/publications/index.html.

Wilson, Karen A. and Colver, Marylou (eds) (1997) *Outsourcing Library Technical Services Operations: practices in academic, public and special libraries*, Chicago, IL, American Library Association, CDI occasional paper 2.

Capital Planning Information Ltd

CPI reports are available from:

CPI @ Instant Library Limited, The Charnwood Wing, Gas Research and Technology Centre, Ashby Road, Loughborough, Leicestershire, LE11 3GS.
Tel: +44 (0)1509 225665
Fax: +44 (0)1509 232748
E-mail: cpi@instant-library.com

Information Management Associates

IMA reports are available from:

Information Management Associates, 28 Albion Road, Twickenham TW2 6QZ.
Tel: +44 (0)20 8755 0471
Fax: +44 (0)20 8755 0471
E-mail: streatfield@compuserve.com.

Chapter 12 Communication strategies

Communication Skills for Library and Information Professionals (1999) training package, London, Library Association Publishing and CHT Solutions.

Leigh, Andrew and Maynard, Michael (1993) *Perfect Communications: all you need to get it right first time*, London, Random House.

Ross, Catherine Sheldrick and Dewdney, Patricia (1998) *Communicating Professionally: a how-to-do-it manual for library applications*, 2nd edn, London, Library Association Publishing.

Index